Raising a Strong Daughter in a Toxic Culture

"If you have a daughter—or two, like me—you need this book! Dr. Meg Meeker's thirty years of being a pediatrician give her the understanding, compassion, and experience to help you build the healthy, loving relationship you both deserve."

— Rachel Cruze, #1 *New York Times* bestselling author and host of *The Rachel Cruze Show*

"Our culture is supposed to be all about empowering women, but really it is strewing our daughters' paths with more pitfalls than any previous generation has had to navigate—from life-threatening bad advice about early sexual activity, to an epidemic of depression (some of it driven by social media), to a near complete misunderstanding of what makes for a happy, productive life. Dr. Meg Meeker is a truth-teller, because she cares about kids—and she knows about kids. She knows how your daughter thinks—maybe even better than you do—and she understands the challenges that parents face. If you want proven advice on how to be a better parent to your daughter, you'll find it here."

— Benjamin Watson, tight end for the Superbowl champion New England Patriots, father of seven children, and author of *The New Dad's Playbook*: *Gearing Up for the Biggest Game of Your Life*

"I devoured this book. I learned so much. As a family doctor, I plan to steal—oops, I meant to say *share*—many of the pearls of wisdom I gained from this indispensable book. My recommendation to parents: Read this book. Now. Then read it again or listen to the audio. Get it in your bones. Then the next time you encounter a tough situation with your daughter, ask yourself, 'What would Dr. Meeker do?' And do it."

— Leonard Sax, M.D., Ph.D., father of a teenage daughter and author of the *New York Times* bestseller *The Collapse of Parenting*

"Daughters need attention. But not just any kind. They need the kind of attention that meets their essential needs. In this book, Meg gives guidance in how to think about those needs and how to meet them. A great help, and a great reminder!"
—Dr. Henry Cloud, psychologist and *New York Times* bestselling author of *Boundaries*

"Honest and emotionally sensitive, this is the best parenting book to help mothers and fathers understand their daughters."
—Erica Komisar, LCSW, author of *Being There*: *Why Prioritizing Motherhood in the First Three Years Matters*

"In this book as in everything she writes, Dr. Meg Meeker offers superb insights for parents and caregivers today. She's a trusted guide through tough topics and a sane voice in confusing times. Don't miss this."
—Maureen Mackey, editor-in-chief of LifeZette

Raising a Strong Daughter in a Toxic Culture

Raising a Strong Daughter in a Toxic Culture

11 Steps to Keep Her Happy, Healthy, and Safe

Meg Meeker, M.D.

BESTSELLING AUTHOR OF *STRONG FATHERS, STRONG DAUGHTERS*

REGNERY
PUBLISHING
A Division of Salem Media Group

Regnery® is a registered trademark of Salem Communications Holding Corporation

Cataloging-in-Publication data on file with the Library of Congress

ISBN 978-1-62157-503-0
ebook ISBN 978-1-62157-571-9

Published in the United States by
Regnery Publishing
A Division of Salem Media Group
300 New Jersey Ave NW
Washington, DC 20001
www.Regnery.com

Manufactured in the United States of America

10 9 8 7 6 5 4 3 2 1

Books are available in quantity for promotional or premium use. For information on discounts and terms, please visit our website: www.Regnery.com.

*To Ainsley, Mary, Maggie, and Elliot, who will be
the next generation of strong women*

Contents

Introduction

How to Do the Right Thing

L et's face it. Daughters can be trouble.

But that's because they're human. You can be trouble too. We all can, because while most of us want to do the right thing—as parents or as kids—we're also tempted to do the wrong thing.

This struggle isn't new. In fact, you can find it all the way back in the Bible. When Saint Paul addressed the Romans, he said something extraordinary. Putting his finger solidly on the conflict each man, woman, and child experiences, he said, "I do not understand what I do. For what I want to do I do not do, but what I hate I do."

As parents, it is critical that we recognize that our sweet, innocent daughters live with the same struggle. Even at two years old, your daughter knows what is generally right and generally wrong. She knows intuitively what she should do (not hit her baby brother in the head with a plastic bat), and yet she does it anyway. She is born with a conscience and from the time she is little, she feels a fundamental tension between doing what is right and doing what is wrong. She contends with her will, her desire for independence, and an impishness that every parent of a young daughter has witnessed.

Your job as a good parent is to understand your daughter, to help her win the battle of conscience, to help her desire what is good and avoid what is evil (no matter how temporarily tempting that evil might seem), to know when disobedience is actually attention-seeking (and many girls' self-destructive behaviors are exactly that), and to guide her through inevitable disappointments and hardships.

It is harder to be a child or an adolescent than it used to be. Our culture is very different from what it was even ten years ago, and it is now often hostile to what is in children's best interests. Girls in the third grade are on diets. Teachers instruct our children that "gender" is "fluid" and that they can choose whether they want to be boys or girls. Some girls begin menstruating in the third grade. Others have "boyfriends" in the fifth or sixth grade. By junior high, most girls are familiar with the term oral sex and may have witnessed it in pornography, if not in fact. They are well-versed in sexually transmitted infections and know about contraception, what an abortion is, and how they should "protect" themselves.

By high school, they will know about drinking and smoking, sleeping around and hooking up, and too many will think that hooking up is something expected of them—even if they hate it (and they do). By their sophomore year if not before, they will know girls who suffer from anxiety and depression—and they will know about kids their age committing suicide.

Our daughters and granddaughters face many threats, but the good news is that we as parents and grandparents have an enormous influence over our children's lives and the decisions they make. And it all begins with something as simple as paying attention and affirming that your daughter's self-worth is inherent—not something she has to earn. It is underlined if you strive to make most of your interactions with her positive, and that can be as easy as spending time with her, letting her know that you take pleasure in being around her, and showing her that you enjoy her company.

Some years ago, I worked with a residential home for troubled teen girls in our area. Most of the girls came to the home angry and defiant. What cured them was adult attention—attention they denied that they wanted or needed. But we gave them adult counselors. They ate with adults, worked with adults, and were taught by adults. In most cases it took about a week, but gradually these girls responded—and appreciated the fact that there were adults who cared about them.

If you want to raise a strong daughter, it begins with showing her that you care. That might be easy early on when she's an infant (or maybe not if she keeps you up half the night crying). When she's an awkward adolescent, it might be harder (or maybe not, since adolescent girls can melt their fathers' hearts). The key thing is to stay engaged, to be there, to understand. This book is the culmination of my thirty years of writing, speaking, teaching, and practicing as a pediatrician. I have tried to keep the notes to a minimum and focus instead on stories that illustrate some of the most important lessons I've learned about kids that can help you and your children do the right thing and have happy, healthy lives together.

Chapter One

Know Her Heart

From the church balcony, I looked down and saw Stefani. She was eight years old, and my gut told me that something was terribly wrong. Her lips looked blue and her movements were sluggish. Though she wasn't my patient, I knew her mother socially, and after the church service I ran down the stairs to get a closer look at the little girl. She was thin, drawn, and pale. Her mother said Stefi was getting "over a recent viral infection that had gone to her heart." She described her daughter's symptoms, and I guessed it was a Coxsackie virus that causes a rash, fever, and—rarely—heart problems. I said I thought Stefani needed further evaluation by her pediatrician. A cardiologist friend of mine quickly got Stefi to the Mayo Clinic, where her parents were told that unless she received a heart transplant soon she would die of heart failure.

Stefi was put on a transplant list and our little church congregation prayed their hearts out for her. She and her parents began the agony of waiting for a new heart to come. And it did.

The selfless parents of Oliver, a seven-year-old boy who had recently died, donated his heart.

Just before she was taken into surgery, Stefi's doctor, Dr. Ackerman, came to see her. They chatted for a while and then the kind doctor prayed with her and asked if she had any questions. "Yes." She said. "Am I going to die?"

He replied, "No! As a matter of fact, I'm going to dance with you at your senior prom!" This was quite a promise from a physician in Minnesota to an eight-year-old in Michigan.

Stefi's surgery was extremely risky, but she came through it well. Transplanting a vital organ from one person to another poses challenges that other surgeries don't. She would face possible organ rejection. She needed to take long-term, powerful drugs to keep her tiny body from rejecting the foreign heart. The drugs included steroids that made her swell like a balloon.

She was on some of these drugs for months and others for years, but I never once heard Stefani or her parents complain about the side effects and everything she had to go through. She remained a kind, soft-spoken, and gentle soul.

Stefani endured her years of treatment with strength and humility. Today she is a nurse—and a very good and compassionate one. She is married and very happy. And her senior prom? She bought a beautiful dress, arrived at the dance, and while mingling with friends, looked up and noticed something remarkable. A few feet from her stood Dr. Ackerman. He had come to dance with Stefi as he had promised ten years earlier. No one at the prom could believe what they saw as the tiny girl with a new heart danced with a surgeon from the Mayo Clinic.

Stefani had lived with two hearts, but one unchangeable personality.

When we speak of a person's heart, we mean so much more than its physical manifestation. We talk of broken hearts, of hearts representing our passions, our sympathies, our truest selves. Our hearts sink in sorrow or soar in exultant joy. And all these feelings can have physical manifestations: our hearts can beat faster with excitement, we can laugh until our ribs hurt, or we can be doubled over with anguish.

Our daughters' hearts are obviously physical, but when we speak of a daughter's heart we speak also of her emotions, character, and spirituality. Her heart—her personality, her core—is constant, even if her *expressions* of her personality, feelings, thoughts, and emotions are not.

Every daughter wants to give four things that come from the "heart." She wants to give love. She wants to form strong attachments. She wants to nurture. And she wants to be loved.

Daughters look to their parents to give them a strong sense of confidence and security in their early years. But as our daughters grow, our perspective as parents should change. For parents it's no longer simply a question of what we can give to our daughters, but of what *they* need to give to others.

You might say, "My daughter refuses to show affection. She treats me with contempt. Far from nurturing her little brother, she's nasty to him. She's even mean to her friends." I know, but read on. No matter how much her needs are hidden or how she behaves outwardly, the desire to give love and be loved still lies deep within her—a constant yearning. And this should give you tremendous hope, because beneath the toddler having temper tantrums, or the angry middle schooler who says she would rather text on her phone than talk to you, or the tattooed teenager who thinks she's a rebel, lies a heart that is still tender. It may be buried under anger, disappointment, sadness, or jealousy—and that's okay. Your job as a parent is to gently chip away at all the barriers she might erect around her heart. But always know that her heart is still there and that she still desires to give love and to be loved. You can't—and don't need to—control everything she does. Life will inevitably leave a few scars on her. But if you understand her constant, fundamental longings, you will eventually understand each other and your relationship will shift— sometimes dramatically—for the better.

Longing #1: To Love

For most parents, showing love for an infant daughter is easy. It's just as easy and natural for a young daughter to express her love for her parents by hugging and kissing them, drawing pictures of them, and feeling ashamed if she breaks parental rules and acts badly. She senses that love is a two-way street—that if she expresses love, she is more likely to receive it.

Three or four times when I was about eight years old, my father brought me to work with him on Saturday mornings. It made me feel special, and those good memories have stayed with me all my life. He let me spin in his enormous desk chair, and when we left his office at the Mass General Hospital we would walk to Harvard Square. He smoked a pipe, and I still love the smell of pipe smoke. He insisted on walking on the traffic side of the pavement, saying that "a man should always walk between you and the road in case something happens. That way, he'll get hurt and you won't."

We would go to a cafe where he ordered coffee, I had hot chocolate, and we both ate baba au rhums (yeast cakes saturated in rum and sugar with whipped cream on top). Truth be told, I never liked them. I was eight. I liked Ho Hos and Twinkies. But I ate them anyway to show my dad that I loved him.

As a child, I was one of the lucky ones. I never doubted my dad's love for me. Whether I gave him a ridiculous drawing or sewed him a dog made of felt, he would always smile graciously and say, "I love it," though I don't recall my crafts staying long in our home.

When your young daughter expresses her love for you, she is using you as a test. Will you love her back, or will you ignore her? Will you return her kiss, or will you turn away? If she brings you a craft she made, will you stop and admire it, or will you wave her away, immersed in your phone?

If you return your daughter's love, she will trust others more and her heart will remain tender. But if her overtures are rejected, she will begin to wall off her heart and she will withdraw, afraid to be hurt again.

Let's be honest—we all fail our kids, at least occasionally. We can't react with jubilation over every gesture of love. But the point is not about being perfect; it's about being present—physically, mentally, and emotionally—and providing an overall experience of love and appreciation. A sincere heart is all your daughter needs. Do your best and let mistakes go.

Longing #2: To Form Strong Attachments

A daughter will reflexively seek to form an attachment to her parents through her first years of life. If you respond well to these overtures and meet her needs, she will feel secure. If, however, you ignore her or become angry with her and do so repeatedly through her first three years, she could have trouble forming healthy attachments later in life.

The idea of "attachment parenting" was popularized by the groundbreaking work of British psychiatrist Dr. John Bowlby, who studied maladjusted children and concluded that a child's failing to form a strong attachment to her mother was a major cause of later emotional and psychological problems.[1]

One of his students, Dr. Mary Ainsworth, expanded on his research and helped confirm his conclusions, becoming one of the most respected figures in the field of child psychology.

The work of Bowlby, Ainsworth, and Dr. Mary Main (one of Ainsworth's students) eventually led to the identification of four different types of attachment.[2]

With *secure attachment*, children trust their parents (or caregivers, like nannies) to respond to their needs, and these children generally go on to greater success in life and have healthy relationships.

Anxious-resistant attachment occurs when a daughter longs for security and safety, but because she fears parental neglect and is not reassured when she receives attention, she clings to her parents, fearful of being separated from them and alone. Ironically, as she clings to them, she really doesn't emotionally depend on them at all.

In *anxious-avoidant attachment*, the child shuts down emotionally to guard herself from pain and even avoids her parents.

Disorganized attachment is when a girl is suspicious of her parents or caregivers, isolates herself from others, and is often aggressive and angry.

Attachment theory has many aspects, but I mention it to underline a simple point: your daughter wants a healthy relationship with you, and that begins by offering her consistent emotional support and attention.

If you do that, you've already gone a long way toward giving your daughter a strong start in life.

Many parents (particularly mothers, especially those who work full-time) worry about forming the right attachment with their child. Some worry whether it's too late to form such an attachment. And others (again, usually mothers) are tempted to become overattached to their daughters. So the million-dollar question is how do you get it right?

Bowlby focused on a child's attachment to her mother because in the 1940s and 1950s when he did much of his work, most mothers remained home with their children while fathers worked outside the home. But times have obviously changed, and fathers can form beautiful attachments with their children. I have witnessed this in many families, including my own.

When our oldest two children were young, my physician husband stayed home with them while I completed my pediatric residency. This took three and a half years, and it bothered me that in the middle of the night the girls wanted him, not me, to comfort them. By circumstance and necessity, they considered him the more loving, compassionate caregiver because he always attended to their needs. He and the kids formed a very healthy attachment. And what about me? I'm still close to all my children, and even help take care of the grandchildren. I made up for lost time by doing the best I could when I could. Healthy attachment isn't rocket science; any parent can do it if they don't overthink it.

Overthinking is a problem that afflicts parents who "over attach" to their daughters; they allow their daughters to become the center of their world, to the exclusion of other relationships. We've all met these parents: the ones who won't stop talking about their kids, who act as if their children's successes are their own. If you don't feel whole without your child, if you measure your own worth in terms of your child's achievements, if you need your child to be present with you most of the time, then you and your child likely have an unhealthy attachment. It's a common problem, and it can happen to the most well-meaning, loving parents. Parents try so hard to do the right thing, but sometimes they go overboard and become dependent on their children's approval and success. The harsh truth is that daughters need parents, but parents can live without their daughters. And all parents should remember that their daughters will eventually leave home. The best way to avoid overattachment is to love your daughter and be there when she needs you, but to go on with your life (and let her get on with hers) and not obsess over your child. That's how children—and their parents—learn to mature in a healthy way.

On the other end of the spectrum are girls who spend the first years of their lives in poorly run orphanages where they are brutally neglected or abused. As infants they learn that crying won't deliver food, attention, or affection. So they stop crying, and over the ensuing months they stop showing emotion at all. As they grow up they might start exhibiting antisocial behaviors because they never formed the positive attachments to parents that give children a sense of security and confidence.

One patient of mine was a nine-year-old girl who had been adopted from a foreign orphanage six months before her visit by a lovely family. She was having trouble at school, couldn't make friends (indeed, she got into fights that she started), refused to participate in school activities, and was uncommunicative or angry at home.

I got the girl to talk to me and discovered that her orphanage was essentially run by the oldest children—the teenagers—who terrorized the younger children, and that some of the girls were sexually assaulted by the teenage boys. It was horrifying, of course, to hear this, but her mother hoped that with a lot of love and support her new daughter would "get over" much of the early pain she had endured.

"I think that the only thing she is comfortable with is anger," her mother said. "She never smiles. She won't let us hug or kiss her. She pulls the hair of her classmates. And she is outright mean to her siblings. As a matter of fact, she went after her twelve-year-old brother recently with a baseball bat and tried to hit him. He was genuinely scared."

Her mother was beside herself and wondered what, if anything, she could do to help her daughter. She went through some very difficult times as her daughter got involved with drugs and sexual activities and almost ran away from home. But her parents stuck with her and employed a counselor to help them. And as their daughter matured through her teen years, she allowed her longing for love to seep out—just a little at a time.

Let me be clear: not all children raised in orphanages or with foster parents develop attachment disorders. I have met hundreds of resilient children who came from terrible home environments and went on to lead healthy and productive lives. My point is a general one: if you feel your daughter might have an attachment disorder, talk with your pediatrician about it.

Longing #3: To Nurture

From the time they're infants, girls are a far more interested in relationships than boys are. Boys like objects that appeal to their eyes. Girls want interaction; they want to communicate and feel and offer affection.

Some psychologists will tell you that daughters prefer dolls to trucks because they have been trained to do so, but they're wrong. And if you watch a young girl play with a doll you can see part of the reason why: she will likely cuddle it, clothe it, and pretend to bathe it. She will use the doll to express her desire to love, to show kindness, and to nurture. Any parent who has raised both a son and a daughter knows that boys have very different interests, skill sets, and ways of communication. And if you want scientific backing for what you can observe yourself, you can look to experts like Dr. Leonard Sax, who wrote the excellent book *Why Gender Matters, Second Edition: What Parents and Teachers Need to Know about the Emerging Science of Sex Differences*.[3] Citing numerous well-done scientific studies, he shows that girls see, hear, and process information very differently than boys do. The differences are not only stark from infancy, but they are physiologically and genetically provable.

Putting dolls aside for a moment, you can get a similar reaction from young girls with stuffed animals. They will pick up the toys and coo over them. Their desire to be kind and to nurture is on display all the time. They see ducklings in the water and want to bring them home so they can raise them. If they find an injured bird, rabbit, or even a toad in the yard, they will feed, house, and care for the animal until it heals. Live with a daughter long enough and her longing to give kindness will surface repeatedly in everything from craft projects given as gifts to crayon pictures expressing her love for you.

When Katherine was eight years old, she was admitted to a nearby children's hospital for eye surgery. Before she was admitted she asked her mother if she could bring her favorite stuffed animal. "Of course," her mother replied.

Katherine's eye surgery went well, and while she was recovering she noticed that most of the other kids in her ward had no stuffed toys to play with—no fuzzy puppy dogs, smooth-haired bears, or cuddly monkeys. "Mom," she said, "I feel badly for these kids."

Katherine was checked out of the hospital, but her concern for the other kids didn't end. She asked her mother if they could buy a few stuffed animals to send back to the hospital, which they did. But that wasn't enough. Katherine solicited donations—from friends, family, even strangers. Within months, her mother had delivered thousands of stuffed animals to hospitals across Michigan—all before Katherine started third grade. Obviously, Katherine was remarkable in making such a big difference at such a young age in so many children's lives. But most girls have within them a similar sense of compassion, even if it exercises itself on a smaller stage.

Girls raised in a happy family generally find it easier to express kindness, but Katherine's story teaches another lesson. Her parents were divorced, yet they kept their relationship amicable as they raised their daughter. Perfection, again, is not the goal, and it is not achievable. The goal is to do the best we can. And if we do, we can help draw from our daughters some of the best gifts they can offer anyone: kindness, patience, and mercy. It's no accident that so many nurses and nursing home caregivers are women.

I got to know a woman named Brenda who worked in the nursing home where my father, who had dementia, lived his last years of life.

Brenda talked a lot about her family. She was a middle child with six siblings and was raised as a good Polish Catholic. Every one of the children had a family job, and she became the family cook.

She remembered her childhood fondly. She talked about hunting with her dad and cooking venison for the family. "My dad is a good man," she would say. "He worked hard, and because of that he wasn't always around, but whenever he was, we knew he was there because he wanted to be with us. That really mattered. It made up for a lot of the times he was away working."

Brenda talked about her mother too. She worked on a local farm harvesting and selling vegetables. "Money was tight, but I always saw my mother make room for another hungry kid or a hurting neighbor. She was kind, she worked hard, and she was tough."

Brenda helped save my father's life. A fire broke out one afternoon in the nursing home kitchen. By the time I arrived, my father and the other residents—who were in wheelchairs and confused—were lined up in the parking lot. Brenda counted them up, realized one was missing, and ran back into the burning building to save a blind woman.

After the fire department had the blaze in hand, I went over to Brenda and asked how she got my two-hundred-pound dad out of his bed, into his wheelchair, and out of the house.

"I'm well-trained," she said, "and my mom always taught me that if someone needs help, you don't think twice. And I guess that just stuck."

"I'd say so," I said. Still, as I looked at her five feet two, 120-pound frame, I had to repeat, "But how did you do it?"

"I picked him up and threw him in the wheelchair."

"No! That's not possible."

"Like I said, I'm well-trained."

I thought that was the understatement of the year.

Brenda saved my dad's life that day because of one thing: she had the heart of a daughter. For years, she had watched and learned, loved and cared. She was raised that way. It didn't matter that both her parents worked. She didn't feel neglected or angry. She knew they cared, and she in turn honed her own sense of caring and compassion.

Longing #4: To Be Loved

Not all truths come from medical textbooks. Some you can extrapolate from literature, philosophy, or the Bible. According to the Bible, God created humanity because he wanted to have a relationship with us. He didn't create us because He thought it was a nice idea. He did it because even He who needs no more than Himself *wanted* us.

Think about that. The most important book in Western Civilization argues that we are made for relationships with God and with each other. At the heart of the Old and New Testament teachings is the idea that God loves us and desires to be close to us. In the Judeo-Christian tradition, the most important thing is not one's career, riches, or worldly achievement. The most important thing is to have rich and rewarding relationships with other people and, of course, with the God who created us.

Doctors—and pediatricians perhaps in particular—know that relationships are vital to the emotional, spiritual, and physical well-being of their patients, and there are plenty of studies that show that churchgoers lead healthier, happier lives—maybe because religious participation helps provide these relationships.[4] Child development research also shows the obvious: that having strong friendships with individuals (not just peer groups) increases an adolescent girl's sense of self-worth and decreases her risk of depression and anxiety.[5] As Aristotle said (long before research proved him right), "In poverty and other misfortunes of life, true friends are a sure refuge. They keep the young out of mischief; they comfort and aid the old in their weakness; and they incite those in the prime of life to noble deeds."[6]

Girls need authentic friendships, and those friendships can be lifesavers. I will never forget a conversation I had with sixteen-year-old Melanie. She was in for a routine checkup but wanted to talk about something else.

"Dr. Meeker, I have a girlfriend who is having a hard time and I don't know what to do about it. It's really bothering me."

"Tell me about it."

"Well, we were at this party with a guy. We shouldn't have been there. His parents were out of town and some of his friends were over—and things happened. I think my friend might be in trouble. If I tell you, you won't tell my folks, will you?"

"Well, Melanie, that depends. If your friend needs serious help, I might need to talk to her parents, and maybe yours. If she is in serious trouble, we both want to help, right?"

"I guess so." She hesitated, but finally said, "Well, here's the thing: people were drinking at the party. Some of the guys were really wasted. It was kind of awful. Anyway, my friend liked one of the guys who was drinking. I thought he was a jerk, but she wouldn't listen to me."

Melanie waited a few moments. "Well, he asked her if she wanted to hook up. She didn't want to, but she didn't want to hurt his feelings. So, she did. They went into another room. I don't think they were the only ones there. She gave him oral sex. That's what girls do. But that's not the worst part." She paused again.

"After it was over, he got up and left her all alone in the room. I guess he told his friends. More guys came to her. They told her they wanted to hook up too. She was scared. About five guys forced her to give them oral sex. Afterwards she came to me and asked me to take her home. She was terribly upset and afraid to face her parents, so she asked if she could stay at my house. She cried most of the night. I just didn't know what to do. It happened last weekend. She's still really upset and doesn't want to go to school. She doesn't want to see those guys. She feels so embarrassed. She cries all the time and won't talk to anyone."

"I assume that her parents still don't know."

"No. Her dad would freak out—and she doesn't want a lecture. She already feels guilty and terrible for having disappointed her parents. I just don't know what to do."

"Melanie, you've done a brave thing. Those boys committed a crime and need to be held accountable, and your friend needs help with the emotional—and maybe physical—consequences of what happened. You've been a good friend. Now I need to call her parents—and yours. It will be hard at first. But it'll be better once we take care of it."

The boys were confronted and charges were filed. Melanie's friend was diagnosed with post-traumatic stress disorder. But thanks to Melanie, she got the help that she needed, and that might have saved her from serious depression—or even suicide. I have seen more than one girl who was driven to self-harm or suicide in similar circumstances.

Your daughter needs friends like Melanie who can stand by her and give her strength—friends in whom she can confide her confusion, her secrets, her darkest fears, and things she might be afraid to share with you. Talking them out can make things better.

Psychologists have long known that girls' friendships are very different from boys' friendships. Girls like to *talk*, to *communicate*. Boys prefer to *do* things together. When girls experience stress, the hormone oxytocin is released. This hormone triggers what is called the "tend and befriend" phenomenon that prompts women to gather with their girlfriends.[7] (The same sort of stressors can prompt the "fight or flight" response in men.) Again, it comes back to the female desire to nurture and to care, to love and to be loved.

As much as she needs the love of friends, your daughter also needs your love. Daughters who don't find love at home will seek it elsewhere, and often dangerously, as Melanie's friend did. Girls who receive love from their parents are confident and secure, have an appropriate sense of self-worth, and are better prepared to say no to bad peer pressure.

It is a basic fact: no girl can thrive if she doesn't feel love. She must be able to give love (which can be as simple as hugging you) and to receive it (receiving a hug or a kiss on the cheek in return). That's why we parents are so critical to our daughters. We must let them know that in all situations we love them. They need our parental attention and affirmation on a regular basis, and they need to feel that they have a few good friends on whom they can count.

Being a parent to a daughter is as simple as recognizing the constant yearnings of her heart and helping her to satisfy them. The good news is that every daughter wants a good relationship with you, her parent. And through the course of this book, I'll try to show you how to make that relationship better.

Chapter Two

Answer Her Four Biggest Questions

Every daughter is born with a deep instinct to find answers to four existential questions. When they are answered, she lives with security, stability, and happiness. The questions are the following:

Where did I come from?
Am I valuable and significant (especially to my parents)?
Is there a moral standard?
Where am I going?[1]

Your daughter's need for answers to these questions is so great that she will look everywhere to find them. She will likely ask you, her friends, her teachers, and yes—even people she doesn't like. What drives her is an innate need to validate her being—to grasp on a primal level that she is valuable, that she is worth being loved, and that she has a purpose.

As parents, we know this about our daughters, but we don't always know how to respond. We want our daughters to feel good about themselves and we want to boost their self-esteem. But we often go about it the wrong way as we focus on achievements and sign them up for stuff. We think if we can help our daughters become concert pianists, then they will feel valuable. Or we think that maybe if they excel at soccer, or become a star of the debate team, or crash the boys' baseball team to prove that they're better than their male peers, *then* they will feel good about themselves. Too many parents of daughters think this way.

But no—the point is not to compete against and beat the boys. Becoming a great soccer player, or debater, or pianist—as worthy as these goals are—will not make your daughter feel valuable. You don't want to trap your daughter into assuming that her inherent value relies on her performing well at a skill or a competition. Kids hate feeling that their parents only give them attention when they succeed at school or extracurricular activities. When this happens, they often feel empty and used and are frequently burned out by their freshman or sophomore year of high school. Ironically, they also suffer from poor self-esteem because they sense that their parents don't really know them for who they are—only for what they do—and if they fail in a game, in a performance, or in a test, then they fail completely.

There are far better ways to teach your daughter that she has innate value. Forget hectic rounds of activities and endeavors—unless you both enjoy them and appreciate them for what they are as a chance to develop skills and talents that are worth exercising—and focus on one thing: teach your daughter that she was created by a loving God. I know that in these secular times it is controversial to say this, but it is true. *Nothing* will give your daughter a deeper sense of self-worth and value than to tell her that God created her for a reason—and I say this as a pediatrician who has seen it in her practice countless times. Girls with this sense of faith are overwhelmingly healthier and happier. And your daughter can learn this idea as young as three years of age. So where do we start?

Question #1: Where Did I Come From?

Children especially, but all of us really, have a burning desire to know where we came from. Young children are always asking the fundamental questions of why and how. How did the moon get in the sky? Why do I have blonde hair rather than black hair? Do angels fly? Children aren't cynical or jaded. They are curious and open. They love fairy tales because they see themselves in the stories, and within those stories they can work out conflicts and drama and learn about life. They instinctively grasp that life is a story and they want to know how their stories started.

Your child's deep need to understand where she came from is not only real—it is reasonable. Many of us have formed answers without really thinking them through based on something as flimsy as a cursory comment made by a friend or a teacher, or something we vaguely remember from a book or a video. We often don't really think about the big questions anymore during the course of our busy lives and are satisfied with barely examined answers.

But this is not good enough for your child. She needs more than simple, superficial answers because understanding where she came from is her basis for understanding the entire world. When she has a well-thought-out answer, she sees her friends, herself, her hardships, her joys, and the world around her very differently. When she has a deep conviction regarding her origin, she has a strong foundation for her life. She is secure. She keenly appreciates her own value and the value of others. She lives with humility and appreciation. Most importantly, she lives with a deep sense that she was created on purpose. She is not an accident or a collection of molecules that randomly came into existence. She is here because she matters. How much different our world would be if everyone understood that they came to be through intention—not by accident.

Oddly enough, teaching a child about her origin is very tricky for most parents. First, we have to collect the courage to have an age-appropriate version of "the Talk" about human reproduction. But truthfully, that's the easy part. It's a lot harder to have the other talk—the one about her ultimate origin and value. Here's what I have found works best—and what doesn't.

What doesn't work is telling your daughter that she is the result of a random colliding of genes and that there is no more to it than that. If you want your daughter to be a nihilist, I guess you could start there. But if you want her to have a sense of self-worth and of the beauty and inevitable mystery of her beginning, you need to say something else; reductionist evolutionism won't cut it. Genetics has its place, but it is an insufficient explanation. As C. S. Lewis wrote:

> An egg which came from no bird is no more "natural" than a bird which had existed from all eternity. And since the egg-bird-egg sequence leads us to no plausible beginning, is it not reasonable to look for the real origin somewhere outside the sequence altogether? You have to go outside the sequence of engines, into the world of men, to find the real originator of the rocket. Is it not reasonable to look outside Nature for the real Originator of the natural order?[2]

I encourage parents who believe in God to explain to their daughter that she was carefully and meticulously crafted by a loving God whom she can get to know but cannot see. She did not come to exist because of an accident or a mistake. On the contrary, *she was wanted*. She was *anticipated*. She was *meant* to be your daughter. Whether by birth, adoption, or foster care, your daughter was designed with a personality unlike any other girl alive and you are thrilled that she is yours.

Daughters who are three can understand this idea and benefit from it. So can daughters who are ten, thirty, or even fifty. It can give them not only a feeling of deep value and significance, but also of hope for their future. I have found that while some parents may feel squeamish or doubtful about the existence and love of God, kids aren't. If you want your kids to grow up to "decide" for themselves what to believe about God, fine. But teach them who He is first, and then let them choose. They will choose for themselves in due course anyway, but in the meantime you will have set them on a healthy track. This is life's biggest question and putting it off and leaving your child uneducated about faith and religion is leaving your child in dangerous ignorance.

When Cassie was five, she was taken away from her parents and placed in foster care because her mother, a single parent, got caught up in using drugs, checked out on parenting, and brought home boyfriend after boyfriend—one of whom sexually abused Cassie on several occasions.

Cassie went through several foster homes, finally landing in one where the mother was kind, but the father was emotionally cold and arguably cruel. He never abused her physically, but he made her feel demeaned and ashamed as a "bad" girl. Still, Cassie spoke warmly of her foster mother, telling me, "She did the best she could. And she loved me. She taught me about God. She told me I was special."

These simple messages penetrated Cassie's heart and kept her filled with hope. "When I was sixteen, I remember something profound changed in me. I honestly can't tell you what it was, but I think I came to know deep in my soul that I was created for something better than what I had known. I think it was God—I'm not sure. But I knew that life was going to get better. Something was going to change."

And change it did. Cassie excelled in sports. She went on to get a soccer scholarship at a Division I university. She did well in college; it was like a fresh start. She told me, "I still can't fully explain what turned my life around, but I honestly think that my foster mother's telling me that I was made for something better, that I was special, sunk in and made a difference, and I came to believe that God was real and that He would help me. And He did."

Cassie is now a happy, grown woman and an amazing mother with a family of her own, and for her that all began with the realization that she was created by a loving God. It gave her a sense of self-worth and of hope—and that's a good beginning for any daughter.

Question #2: Do I Have Value and Significance?

You might think it is obvious that your daughter is valuable because she's a human being. But she approaches this question more honestly than most adults do, because when it comes right down to it, many of us don't really believe that we have inherent worth. We believe instead that our worth comes from what we do: our success, our achievements, our good character, our ability to be kind and love others. These are laudable and important things, but ultimately our worth—and your daughter's sense of self-worth—should not come from what she does or what others think of her. It should not be extrinsic; it should be intrinsic. Of course it feels good, at least temporarily, *if* we are liked, *if* we succeed at getting good grades, *if* we make money, *if* we get a good job. But those are all *ifs*. And even if they all come true, many successful people are emotionally miserable. No matter how successful we are, it is not enough because we crave a deeper and more satisfying way of understanding our significance.

Your daughter certainly does. One of her greatest cravings is to be affirmed for who she is, to be assured that she has intrinsic value simply for being who she is—regardless of what she does in the world.

Most of us have a hard time accepting this because all of us—teachers, friends, parents—think in terms of performance and achievement, of pushing kids to do more, to be better at something. Many of us come by this impulse honestly because we never felt affirmed by our parents. So we hover over our daughters to make sure they have high self-esteem, and we mistakenly think that they will get that self-esteem from their achievements.

They won't. I know that this might be hard for some parents to accept, but teaching your daughter that she has intrinsic value because she was created by a loving God will do more for her sense of self-worth than any measure of worldly success.

Don't get me wrong—helping our daughters to excel at something, encouraging them to find good friends, teaching them to be kind to others, and counseling them on matters of good character are important and worthy goals. But if they are all we give our daughters, then we fail them. Why? Although accomplishments can build self-confidence and provide useful discipline, they ultimately cannot provide consolation for our inevitable frustrations, occasional failures, or the deepest longings of our hearts. You daughter needs your love most of all; she needs to know that your love is unconditional. If she is taught that she was created for a purpose by a loving God, she will have the greatest consolation she could possibly have through all of life's travails. She will be inoculated against some of our culture's most destructive messages—the ones that tell her that she must be thin, beautiful, popular, or sexy, or that she must go to an Ivy League school or break a glass ceiling by becoming a CEO to have any real worth. No—her worth comes from the simple fact that she is a human being created in the image of God. Teach her that, and the rest of her life's accomplishments will be what they should be with the benefits of a life well-lived. But it is the life itself that counts.

Teaching your daughter this simple lesson will be harder than it might seem because you'll have the weight of her peers, screens, magazines, movies, and a whole lot more arguing against you, telling her instead all the things she needs to do to be popular and attractive. Some of them are downright dangerous—anything from extreme diets, to sexual activity, to (these days) getting tattoos. The world can be a scary place for kids; you know it and I know it. In fact, I remember a girlfriend saying to me in the 1980s, "I'm not going to have kids. The world is too scary and I'm afraid of what it might do to them." I hear the same sentiment all the time from millennials today. But there is a lot you can do. The very fact that you are her mom or dad makes you the greatest influencer on your daughter's life. You are invaluable when it comes to instilling and supporting her sense of self-worth.

When I ask older girls and teens in my practice what their two biggest challenges are, they answer quickly: being thin enough and sexy enough. They feel pressure to lose weight and to be sexy or sexually active because they think it will make them popular. Many girls believe that they are not good enough the way they are, and they will grab at anything that promises to make them feel better about themselves.

Many moments in our daughters' lives are brutal. Aside from the usual challenges—everything from peer pressure to broken hearts—they live in a toxic culture full of pornography, confusion about healthy sexuality, and even perhaps educationally instilled doubts about their own "identity." Some of the threats to our daughters' well-being you can control, but others you can't. But a common thread through them all is that your daughter's sense of her inherent value is her best defense against bad peer pressure, low self-esteem, depression, and despair.

Consider this: when your eight-year-old daughter finishes at the back of a pack in a school race, she might feel embarrassed, her self-confidence might fall, or she might—if she has an appropriate sense of her own innate self-worth—say with precocious, optimistic maturity, "It was just a race; I'll try to do better next time."

Or consider this: Your fifth-grade daughter is facing a school math test. She has studied hard, but she still doesn't understand some of the fundamental concepts. If she's afraid of looking stupid, she might try to cheat by peeking at the answers of her neighbor who is good at math, and almost assuredly she will compound that error in judgment by lying about it. She knows that cheating is wrong and she will feel guilty. She doesn't want to be a cheater and she doesn't want to lie, but she also doesn't want to disappoint you with bad grades. But if you've taught her that her value doesn't lie in being a math whiz (although you still want her to do the best she can), she will be more likely to follow her conscience instead of cheating because she will know that there is no guilt or shame in doing her best while recognizing that math is a struggle for her. You want your daughter to know that such weaknesses or setbacks do not demean her as an individual or endanger her relationship with you or with God.

In her teen years, the stakes can get higher. If she lacks a sense of inherent self-worth, it could divide you from your daughter as she tries to find extrinsic affirmations of her value. Most days you might barely see her because she leaves for school at seven o'clock in the morning and has choir practice after school, or piano practice, or sports practice, or a performance, or a game. And performances and games also can happen on the weekends. Sometimes you can go with her, but other times you can't. And even when she is at home, you might find that she mostly stays in her room. You figure that's all right because that's what teens do, so you leave her alone to text with her friends.

The explosion might come on Sunday night—the only night that your family can enjoy dinner together. She refuses to join in, accuses you of trying to control her, and instead goes out to a friend's home.

Unfortunately, this becomes a habit and she grows more distant, sullen, and talks only with her friends—not with you. A boyfriend appears—exactly the sort you've warned her against—and they spend all their free time together. You feel her slipping away, and you grieve, and you worry, but your friends reassure you that this is normal teenage behavior and that she will outgrow it. But something inside of you knows they are wrong. You might have the sickening realization that your daughter lacks a sense of self-worth and is seeking validation not from you, but from others—and that is a dangerous thing. And you're right.

This is a scenario that I have seen countless times over the years— and it doesn't matter whether the teens in question were considered good kids or troublemakers, good students or bad, wealthy or poor. The bottom line is that when your daughter refuses to spend time with family or siblings, there is trouble in her heart. She knows it, and you know it, but neither of you knows what to do about it.

And here's how it often starts: she feels insecure, she feels like a failure compared to her friends, she is uncomfortable with herself, she becomes uncomfortable around you, and she might even blame you for what she sees as her shortcomings in looks or popularity.

She feels a bit lost in her busy schedule and afraid, because every practice, every performance, every game could expose her as a failure— not as good as her friends. And what if they make fun of her? She feels overwhelmed, but she doesn't want to say so because she knows you are excited for her, and she wants to please you.

But as her busy schedule keeps her from home, she tries to bond more closely with her friends, and she feels a growing distance from you and her siblings. She senses that this is wrong; she wants to be tightly knit to her family, and she wants to be missed when she's not there. But given her lack of an innate sense of self-worth and her focus on external achievements, she focuses more and more on receiving approval from others. Performance has taken over her life to the point that she feels she is losing her connection to you. In order to get your attention, she feels she needs to keep performing—getting the good grades, scoring goals, playing in concerts, being popular with the right friends. And if she fails, she feels that she may not be wanted at home—or anywhere else. Does anyone really want her company?

Halfway through high school, she feels exhausted and knows there must be more to life than just doing a lot of stuff. Rarely spending time at home, rarely eating meals with the family, rarely having anything more than the most superficial of conversations with you, she turns to her peers: her soccer buddies, her classmates, and the boy who pays attention to her.

They take your place, but the problem is that their attention really isn't what she wants. Deep down, even though she might deny it, she longs for positive attention from you. She longs to reconnect with you.

If you're a mother, you share your daughter's desire to communicate, to love, and to be loved, and you can restart the conversation. If you're a father and you spend time with your daughter, then you can become her shield. If you have a good relationship with your daughter and if you have taught her that she is intrinsically valuable, she will be far less likely to engage in risky behaviors or become sexually active in high school. The fact is that most teen girls become sexually active *not* because they want sexual pleasure, but because they want male attention and intimacy and lack a good relationship with their father.

The battle for a teenage daughter's heart can be intense. She needs your time and your attention; she misses family dinners, car rides, walks, and conversations. If she becomes distant, there's a reason why. *Every* hurting teenage girl I have seen over the past thirty years believes that no one cares enough to listen or pay attention to her. This belief often develops after she gets overly involved in activities that keep her away from home and that lead her to the conclusion that her family is more interested in how she performs than in spending time with her.

I know this can be confusing for us parents. We try to do what we believe is best for our children. We follow the lead of other parents, teachers, and coaches. We want our daughters to have good self-esteem (which we believe comes through excelling at school or extracurricular activities), and we want them to succeed in order to get a good job and make lots of money so they can live comfortably. But we miss what is most important to them; we miss that what they long for and need from us is our time and attention. When they don't get them from us, our daughters conclude that something is wrong with them—that they aren't lovable or even likeable.

Remember that your daughter, like all children (including teens), is egocentric and feels that she is responsible for all the things that happen in her life. Even if she blames you in anger, in truth she will feel that she is somehow at fault. This is important to remember for several reasons, but one of them is that however much you think she craves the approval of her peers, you should know that the approval she really craves is *yours*. Your attention and love can make all the difference.

If she's worried about her weight—as so many girls are—you can reassure her that her body will continue to change as she grows, that balance and moderation are the rule in diet and exercise, and that her value to you, as your daughter, has nothing to do with a number on a scale.

Diet extremism can be dangerous, and we'll talk more about that later, but the risks of premature sexual activity are even more dangerous. The two are unfortunately linked because girls who don't see themselves as thin and "hot" can believe they have no value at all—certainly not to boys—and seek to find that missing value by becoming sexually active. Most teens assume that most teens are sexually active. This is a horrible misconception, but it is propagated because the many girls who are not sexually active stay quiet and the ones who are sexually active boast about it to gain more attention and highlight how desirable they are. If your daughter lacks self-esteem, she may be vulnerable to the taunts of her peers who might accuse her of being prudish, unpopular, uncool, and not grown-up.

If a girl's sense of self-worth comes from her peers—and who doesn't want to be popular, liked, and accepted?—she will feel the need to act like them. The good news is that you can have a lot of influence over your daughter's choice of friends, and that can be crucially important. Girls with good friends feel more secure and are far more likely to stay away from smoking cigarettes or marijuana, steer clear from the wrong kinds of parties, and hold back from dating boys who only want sex. In short, helping your daughter surround herself with good friends is one of the best things you can do to protect her from bad influences, keep her out of trouble, raise her self-esteem, and maintain her sense of personal significance.

Recently, I saw a notably joyful seventeen-year-old patient. She had a great relationship with her mother, her father, and even her younger brother. She was applying to colleges and was very articulate. Before she left, I asked her what the secret to her happiness and success was. She thought for a moment and said, "Great parents and having the right friends. I've never really felt pressure to do stupid stuff because my friends and I stick together in our decision to avoid bad things. We give each other a lot of encouragement."

Good friends can help our daughters feel popular and reaffirm their commitment to forming good habits and making wise decisions. But the wrong friends can take girls in a disastrous direction. One place where girls often find the wrong friends is on social media.

Acceptance: The Lure of Social Media

Whatever their benefits for some girls, many girls find that social media platforms create havoc and pain in their lives. I often tell my patients that Instagram, Facebook, and Snapchat are "show-off" platforms. They're not about communicating with friends; they're about boasting how one girl's life is better than another's, and it leaves many girls feeling inadequate, dissatisfied, and depressed.

So what is a parent to do? We can tell our daughters that social media popularity is not real popularity, that their place in our hearts has nothing to do with social media, that show-off social media tweets and posts are shallow, that paying attention to social media is a waste of time, and that the real value of one's life is in living well in the real (not virtual) world.

Social media makes it even more important that you teach your daughter that she has innate dignity as a woman both created by God and loved by her parents. Tell her that—especially *before* she's tempted to go on social media—and she will benefit enormously. It will be her shield and her armor in a social media world full of bullying and false values.

The girls who get into trouble on social media are the ones who don't know the plain truths about their innate dignity and worth. They are the ones who become insecure, who fear they are unloved, and who spiral into negative behaviors merely to get attention or in vain attempts to find the affirmation they feel is otherwise lacking in their lives. When teen girls are miserable, disconnected from their families, and acting out in self-destructive ways, their parents sometimes come to me and want to send their girls off to a place that will fix them. They look for programs where girls will be provided with counselors and challenged to do things that they thought they couldn't—like rappel down a mountainside or take a zipline over a gorge— all in an effort to build their self-esteem. Two months of that, they think, and maybe their daughters can come home and resume a more positive life.

There are some great programs out there and I don't mean to diminish their importance. But any good psychologist will confirm that resolving your daughter's hurt begins with you, her parents. Your daughter's sense of rejection, depression, and anxiety is linked to you, and her recovery will begin when you dive in and get involved in the healing process. It starts with spending time with your daughter and listening to her. By listening you'll find where your connection with your daughter went wrong or was severed, and you'll discover how you can repair it. Only then can you begin the process of healing by affirming that she has intrinsic value to you and to God—and you can do that not just by telling her, but also in subtle ways by *showing* her.

I vividly remember my father insisting—over my teenage objections every summer—that we spend two weeks in Maine hiking and camping.

None of our friends' fathers made them do something so stupid, my siblings and I complained, and we sometimes even gave our parents the silent treatment.

But not long after I left home for college, I realized how smart my father had been. He knew that our family bonded during that time in the woods. The shared memories, the long chats—all of it strengthened us, and even healed us from the pressures of the rest of our lives.

Those two weeks were a continual reminder to me that I fit somewhere, that I was welcomed and wanted. Whether I excelled or not, I belonged to a family and we belonged to each other. I miss my father and mother today, who have both passed away, but my three siblings and I are extremely close. My brothers, like my husband, are men I can rely on. And my sister and I are kindred spirits. We talk a few times per week and when something big happens, she is the first person I call. My father, through his insistence on family holidays, helped knit our family closely together, and by doing so he helped teach us that we were all invaluable parts of a greater whole—that we were morally significant and were made to be joyful and confident.

It is easy to forget sometimes what an indelible influence we are on our children. Your daughter's identity forms early in life by watching you—her parents—and seeing whether you smile or frown at her. It continues throughout her life at home; every affirmation and every criticism is registered. Children and teens are egocentric. They believe that life revolves around them, they are sensitive to parental approval or disapproval, and they feel they are responsible for their parents' moods (which is why children so often blame themselves when their parents divorce). As parents, we shape our children's identities far more than our culture does. You should worry *slightly* less about the television shows your daughter watches and work much harder to spend quality time with her—time is the most powerful tool you have to shape her future.

Your daughter will crave your approval, but empty flattery won't cut it. She will know when you are sincere and when you are not. If you tell your daughter she is good at the piano when she isn't, she'll know you're lying. So don't. She will know when you are chronically disappointed in her, regardless of how often you tell her otherwise. The very fact that she innately senses truth from falsehood is yet another reason why she needs to know she has intrinsic value—for all those times she fails, for all those talents she doesn't have, for the inevitable times when she thinks she has disappointed you academically or in some other way.

That's also why it is imperative that all mothers and fathers take inventory of a few things. If we are to succeed in teaching our daughters that performance really doesn't determine their value to us, we need to really believe this to be true. Sadly, many of us aren't really sure. We, too, are enmeshed in the performance trap. We inevitably bring the experience of our own childhood, good or bad, to our new role as parents. Because of that, it can be helpful to do some soul-searching. Here's where we can start.

First, write down how you felt about yourself as a child. Did you feel loved, encouraged, strong, and important? Or did you live with chronic shame, fear, or disgust about yourself? You need to know because the chances are good that *you will project some or all of these feelings onto your daughter.*

Second, be honest about your beliefs and feelings about your daughter. Again, these may be heavily influenced by your beliefs about yourself as a child. If you believe she will grow up to be a failure, she will. If you believe that she is a gift given to you and that your job is to nurture, care for, and guide her as she figures out who she is, then she will come to believe that she is valuable. She will see herself as a gift and you as the treasure keeper. And I guarantee you that every girl wants to feel like a gift to her parents.

Sadly, every day our daughters are bombarded by toxic messages. They are led to believe that their value comes from how many "likes" they get on social media and how "sexy" they are. And it begins in elementary school. I had a father recently tell me that his daughter in *kindergarten* had received a note from a classmate telling her she was "hot." That's the way our culture is going; our job as parents is not to let our children get swept away by it.

Our daughters are young, impressionable, and desperately want to fit in with their friends. Too many parents assume that their daughters know where their real value lies—but they don't. They need to be taught, and it is the job of her parents to do the teaching.

Here are truths that each of us must teach our daughters:

- You are valuable because you are my daughter
- You have significance as a human being and are loved by me—and by the God who made us
- You are valuable because you can love
- You are valuable because you are a unique individual with inherent gifts (and your value lies in the fact that you have them, not in how you use them)

Your value does NOT come from:

- Whether you are popular, or how many "friends" follow or like you on social media, or what others say or think about you
- What you look like—or whether you are "sexy"

To do this, simply do what comes naturally as a mother or a father—be affectionate with your daughter. But also focus on her character—her courage, patience, tenacity, kindness, and empathy—instead of how skilled she is at playing the piano or performing in a recital or ballet class. Practice complimenting her character rather than focusing on how well she did or didn't do in these things. Leave her in no doubt of your—and God's—unconditional love for her. Your daughter wants to hear from you; she values what you say. All we need to do is be bold enough to tell her the truth: that she is significant because she is your daughter—a human being of innate, intrinsic value that was created by you and by God for a purpose.

Question # 3: Does Morality Exist?

When we jettisoned traditional moral standards and replaced them with moral relativism, we did an enormous disservice to our daughters.

Daughters are born with an inherent sense of right and wrong, but that doesn't mean they will always do what they know to be right. Conscience can be challenged by will, and sometimes it kicks in only after a child experiences guilt (like when the eleven-month-old child toddles over and hits the family dog over the head with a toy and remorse kicks in after the dog whimpers and runs).

The conflict between conscience and will might seem perverse, but from a psychological perspective it makes sense. Healthy development in girls requires that they move from dependence to independence as they mature. The struggle is easy to see in things like temper tantrums. When a child's will comes into conflict with her limitations, she becomes frustrated. She might feel guilty about it afterward, but in the moment her frustration overwhelms her developing conscience and she throws a fit.

Teenagers have temper tantrums for much the same reasons. When their conviction that they are ready to set their own curfew, discipline themselves to study well, navigate friendships in a mature manner, and behave responsibly is met with failure, they become frustrated and angry with themselves. So they implode—in front of you, of course, because you are the safe person. You are the one who won't call them crazy and psycho like their friends would.

Their frustration and anger with themselves can make them yell, cry, run out of the house, and slam doors. Don't take it personally and don't blame yourself, because just as kids think the world revolves around them, parents often see their children's misbehavior as proof that they have failed in their parental role. But this often isn't true. Some of these internal battles have nothing to do with us; they're just part of growing up and of your daughter's developing understanding of her capacities and limitations. And the more strong-willed your daughter is, the more intense these challenges might be.

I recently spoke with a mother who was at her wits' end with her very strong-willed two-year-old daughter. Her daughter hated being confined to her car seat, had learned how to unbuckle it, and insisted on sitting where she wanted. Her mother would pull over to the side of the road, reprimand her young daughter, strap her back in, and drive away— only to have her daughter free herself all over again.

This is one strong-willed child—and personally, I love strong-willed kids because they are the ones who are going somewhere in life. The challenge for their parents is to keep them safe and on the right track until that happens, as well as to redirect their stubbornness so that it works for them—not against them.

What is going on inside this young girl's mind as she unbuckles herself? She knows that she isn't supposed to do it and that she will get into trouble if she does. But she doesn't care. Her will dominates her conscience. It would be foolish and pointless to try to reason with her and say, "Rachel, you are a good girl, but you need to listen to me. I know what is best for you and you must stop unbuckling your seatbelt." Instead, you need to be practical and find a better way to keep her secure. Buy a different car seat. Add an extra strap or buckle. And then comes the hard part: let her scream when she can't get out of the car seat. Put some ear plugs in and drive on. Or turn up the radio. Endure the tantrum until it goes away. Win her battle for her now, and she will learn how to win it for herself when she is older.

As your daughter matures, reason can play a larger role. Talk to her about her internal struggles between knowing what is right and doing, sometimes, what is wrong. Show her that when she lets her bad instincts win, bad things happen—not always immediately, but in the long term. As you have these discussions, you can put more and more responsibility on her shoulders. When it comes to changing her behavior, this often works better than if you simply bring the hammer down with strict discipline. Sometimes you need to do that too, but first recruit her mind and will into doing what she knows to be right.

My friend Dr. Henry Cloud, coauthor of *Boundaries*,[3] is a psychologist and a father. He does something brilliant with his teenage daughters.

He has weekly family meetings where they talk about things like school-work, curfews, friendships, expectations, good choices, bad choices, and consequences. He puts responsibility on his daughters. "You can go out tonight," he says, "but just remember to follow the rules. If you break curfew, you'll put me in a tough spot. I'll have no choice but to implement consequences and I'd rather avoid that." This is a great way to teach your daughters to be responsible and make the right choices. It puts the onus on them while giving them a clear direction for what is right and wrong. Their sense of self-worth increases as they see themselves making moral decisions.

A child's sense of morality is intuitive, but lacks experience. The child offsets that by watching you. So beware of what you show them, because they will follow your lead—initially, at least. If they see you express frustration by shouting, they will likely shout when they're upset. If they see you indulge in "little white lies," they will do the same. If they see you act rudely, they will think that's how you assert yourself.

Recently, I had an eleven-year-old girl tell me to "shut up," and her mother gave her a quirky smile. Neither appeared embarrassed. Another mother might have removed the child from the room, given her a talking to, and made the girl say that she was sorry. But this mother implied that she approved of her daughter's behavior.

On another occasion, I was examining a six-year-old girl with her father in the room. He said something forgettable and inconsequential, but the daughter reprimanded him angrily: "Dad, shut up—that is so rude! Don't say that to me again!"

The father replied, "I'm sorry I made you angry and that you had to speak to me that way."

I was stunned.

We shouldn't accept rudeness in our children—and of course we shouldn't be rude ourselves. But many adults, I'm afraid, no longer agree on what is acceptable or unacceptable behavior—let alone what is moral or immoral—and that's a big problem for our daughters. What is merely annoying for us is confusing for them.

It starts because kids assume that what adults tell them is true. If your daughter sees someone misbehave on the playground and reports that child to the teacher, only to have the teacher discount the behavior as unimportant, she is confused because the teacher's inaction conflicts with her own innate sense of right and wrong. But she will accept the teacher's verdict. Today, children are often confused by the official sanction given to "transgenderism," which conflicts with their sense of reality—let alone right or wrong. As they get older and become teenagers, their moral judgement can be swayed if they find that adults have different opinions from those that they had taken for granted.

This is why providing your daughter with a sound foundation of morality is so important. Not only can it protect her against those who would lead her astray, but morality (and I speak of what I know: traditional Judeo-Christian morality) affirms the dignity and sanctity of human life. It tells us that we are to love our neighbor as ourselves, to care for the less fortunate, and to adhere to a moral standard that we did not invent, but that was given to us by a loving God. He gives our lives meaning, value, and purpose. No one can bestow a higher worth on us than to be made in the image of God. If we teach our children to settle for lesser standards of behavior and morality, it can become a serious problem when they grow older and lead them to make very bad life choices.

Encouraging your daughter to invent her own moral standard won't work either because no subjective morality can teach her that she has supreme value—regardless of her accomplishments, failures, or differences. It will do nothing to cushion her inevitable disappointments. On the other hand, giving your daughter an objective standard of morality will remind her that she was born from her parents' love and the love of God. That is the best guiding light you can give her.

Question #4: Where Am I Going?

We all worry or wonder about the next days or years of our lives. Beneath those thoughts lies a hope that life will get better. Our daughters, who have less experience than we do, can be anxious about the future. Many of the challenges they face (making new friends, changing schools, dating) will be faced for the first time. Some girls who lack confidence become so obsessed with what the next days or months hold that they become full of anxiety and cannot live fully and happily in the moment.

Our job as parents is to help our daughters know that they can handle life. We must reassure them that they can get through mean comments, rejection from friends, failed tests, or not making the swim team. Many of us, with good intentions, get upset when bad things happen to our daughters and blame bad teachers or coaches. But all of us have experienced failures or been on the receiving end of cruelty, and your daughter will be no different.

One of the greatest gifts we can give our daughters is the belief that no matter what life throws at them, they can handle it. When we continually react to their troubles as though they are innocent victims, we cripple them. Yes, they may be victims of horrible events. But showing them that we feel sorry for them lets them believe that they are weak and powerless. Instead, we need to show them that bad things happen that are beyond their control, and that's okay.

A friend of mine, John O'Leary, was caught in a terrible house fire when he was nine. Over 90 percent of his body was burned and he should not have survived. Miraculously, he did survive after spending months in the hospital.

When he arrived home, his mother made his favorite meal. He, his siblings, and his parents sat down for a celebration dinner. His sister was seated beside him. His hands had been burned off and there were nubs at the ends of his wrists. He managed to get a fork wedged between the nubs and tried in vain to stab the food on his plate. Seeing this and feeling sorry for him, his sister leaned over to help, stabbing his food on her fork. John's mother cried out, "Stop it! He can do it by himself!"

John was humiliated and angry with his mother because it was hard for him to adapt to his life-altering challenges. She refused to feel sorry for him because she knew that this would cripple him further, and she wanted him, however difficult it would be, to learn to take care of himself. Her belief in John and his tenacity worked, and he now credits her with helping him move forward to achieve great success in his life.

We all need hope for the future—and hope is something we sometimes need to earn. We earn it through our own efforts (as John did), through our confidence that we can handle what life throws at us (which is affirmed by parents and earned by experience), and through our faith that in the end God will save us because He loves us and wants us with Him.

Be ready for your daughter's big questions, because with the right answers you will give her the hope and confidence that she needs.

Chapter Three

Mom: Mentor, Ally, Glue

I first met Kristine in a filthy cinder-block room in the Dominican Republic. She was draping a camouflage green net over her bunk to keep out spiders and other insects. She made her bed with military precision. And she was as happy as if she was settling into a Five-Star Hotel. "This is going to be such a wonderful trip," she said to no one in particular, but it certainly made the rest of us women near her bunk more optimistic.

I had never slept in a room like this before. It was sweltering, and the six of us were dripping wet—partly from the heat, partly from anxiety. Outside of our temporary home stood several sixteen-year-old "guards" holding automatic rifles. I was frightened for my own safety and that of my teenage daughter, who came along with me on this medical mission trip.

Still, I loved Kristine's optimism—actually, I needed it. Part of me was ready to repack my two pairs of surgical scrubs and tennis shoes and get back home. I'm sure I wasn't alone—except of course for Kristine. I marveled at her calm demeanor and enthusiasm. She introduced me to her daughter Rachel, who confided in me that her mom was seventy-three. I was dumbfounded. Grandmother Kristine was faring a whole lot better than I was. She didn't mind the bugs, or the "bathrooms" without plumbing, or the sixteen-year-old guards. She had been here many times before and took it all in stride.

Every morning of our two-week trip we boarded a rickety school bus and were driven to a village with no electricity and no running water where we met hundreds of beautiful men, women, and children who had waited in line for hours in ninety-degree weather to see one of us doctors. Every morning, Kristine was among the first to unpack our medicines, move exam tables and benches into place, and welcome our patients. She was always ready to help and was always in a good mood—despite the trying circumstances. Some of our patients were starving, some had badly infected open wounds, and some were not likely to make it. But through it all, Kristine never appeared rattled or frustrated. Her daughter Rachel told me that her mother made a point of silently or quietly praying for us and our patients. I know that Kristine had more stamina than Rachel or I did, though we were both thirty years her junior. At the end of a hard day, Kristine always looked forward to the next.

Rachel was one lucky woman to have a mother like that. In fact, she made me feel like a failure with the example I was setting for my own daughter—who, I noticed, chagrined, comforted, and encouraged me more than I did her. If nothing else, I thought Kristine set a good example for me of what I should be like at seventy-three.

One evening, I told Rachel, "Your mother is extraordinary. I don't know how she withstands the heat, let alone keeps smiling no matter what happens."

"She is extraordinary," Rachel replied. "She has been doing this for many years. When I was younger, I thought she was crazy. You know what I mean—one of those Bible-thumping, crazy Christians. I don't know why I thought that because she never threw the Bible in our faces, and she certainly never boasted about her faith. Do you see how calm and kind she is to everyone here? That's the way she's always been at home."

I saw pride on Rachel's face, as well as sadness—and I soon found out why.

"Growing up with my mom was hard at times. My dad died when I was young, but my mom was always there for my brother, sister, and me. She didn't complain. She never felt sorry for herself. I think it was her generation. You know, they didn't discuss their feelings. But I hurt for my mom. As I got a little older, I gave her a really hard time. As a teenager, I argued with her, called her names, and let my anger rip. I was never really mad at her. I was just angry because of the struggles we had without a father—and I didn't want her to have to sacrifice as she was either. I know it's odd, but I gave her such a hard time because I felt sorry for her. Go figure.

"Now, as a grown woman, I have come to appreciate her like I never did when I was a kid. My mom showed me how to accept life and people because she did. She showed me how to love people—especially people I didn't like. Like I said, she was never preachy. She was just loving, especially toward us kids and her family. And I honestly don't think I ever met anyone who didn't say nice things about my mom. She makes me proud. She taught me how to live well. She imparted to me what is important in life—and what isn't."

Our conversation took place several years ago, and Kristine has since passed away. But in my mind's eye I will always see her smiling, walking quietly among the sickest of the sick, praying silently for everyone—a mother to her daughter and to us all.

Some psychologists and pundits will tell you that mothers are unnecessary, that "all kids need is a loving home with one or two loving people." Yes, kids need a loving home, and yes, they need loving parents. But mothers and fathers are both irreplaceable; each brings something unique and each provides a different role model that a child needs and wants. When Rachel mourned the loss of her father, she needed her mother all the more.

If you want the best academic research on mothers translated into layman's terms, you can find it in the book *Being There: Why Prioritizing Motherhood in the First Three Years Matters*[1] by Erica Komisar, a psychoanalyst and social worker who had the audacity to say that mothers need to put their children's needs first. I highly recommend her book to any parent interested in understanding the importance of maternal attachment and what children need in order to grow up emotionally healthy. We know from research that mothers bond more easily with their young children than fathers do, are more responsive and empathetic, and are vital to an infant's sense of security.

Much of the research focuses on the hormonal or biochemical reactions that lie behind these behaviors, but I can also apply my own thirty years of experience as a pediatrician to tell you what I've learned from my patients. Children see mothers and fathers as being very different. They believe that a mother's love is non-negotiable and inherent in who she is, while a father's love must be earned. If a father chooses to love his daughter, she feels special. But a mother's love is something she feels she can always fall back on. It's a security blanket—and that belief is entirely psychologically reasonable.

When a child is born, her mother is her introduction to life, love, and security. If that is missing, it is a huge vacancy. As a teen once told me, "If your mom doesn't love you, then good luck. No one will love you." Even a teen who thinks she doesn't like her mother will be devastated if her mother, the one person whose love she can always trust, pulls it away. Daughters see their mothers as offering security, comfort, dependability, and love, and if that relationship is strong, she will hold her mother closer than her most devoted friend.

Glue

Josie remembers being frightened at night when she was four; she was afraid to go to sleep, afraid her world might end. She felt like her life was divided between a daytime life of joy and a nighttime life of fear. I asked Josie, now twenty, to explain.

"When I got home from school my mom would take me places—ballet, piano, or sometimes even out shopping. We had so much fun. I remember driving around with her and talking about so much. But there was always something wrong, something that bothered me terribly, but I was afraid to ask her about it."

She paused for a long moment before saying, "My mom is absolutely amazing. She's the glue in our family. My dad usually came home from work around dinnertime. He was quiet. He read. I never remember him putting us to bed or anything like that. Don't get me wrong—he was always nice to us kids. He never raised his voice. We knew we were important to him. But later, after we went to bed, I could hear my parents arguing. At the beginning, I would sometimes stand at the balcony to listen, but then I stopped because I was too scared. That was my night-time life: my parents yelling, hearing my mom cry."

She had tears in her eyes as she continued: "My mom later told me that my dad struggled with mental illness. He was trying hard to get control of it. He talked to her about it. I think in some peculiar way she understood him. With her help, he tried to pull out of it, and sometimes he did. Psychiatrists in the beginning didn't know what to do with him. They gave him Valium, which he didn't like because it put him to sleep. He had a very demanding job, and he drank to deal with the emotional or mental pain he felt and the pressure, even though he knew it was bad for him and everyone in our family. He went to AA and to one doctor after another.

"This went on for years, and I didn't know what was going on until just a couple of years ago when my mom told me. Anyway, a doctor finally put my dad on a new medication that worked for him. He was like a different person. He didn't rage. He didn't drink. I'm not saying he was nice all the time, but he was never mean; he didn't yell. And one day he asked if we could talk. I'll be honest—I was scared. I had never really had a one-on-one conversation with my dad. On top of that, I was just afraid of him.

"We sat in the living room, and when he started to talk, he began to cry. I had never seen my dad cry before. I was stunned. I didn't know what to do. I just sat there and stared at him. I'll never forget what he said that day. 'Josie,' he said, 'I have done some horrible things to you and our family—especially to mom.' He told me he didn't want to use it as an excuse, but he had been diagnosed with manic depression. He had tried hard to overcome it, but he knew that he had been out of control at times. He asked if I could forgive him for what he had done. I didn't know what to say. No one had ever asked for my forgiveness before. And this was my dad. I said, 'Well, I don't know. I'll see.' That was the best I could do. I got up and left him there in the living room."

I asked Josie, "Was he sincere?"

"Yes, absolutely. He was a different man."

"Did you ever forgive him?"

"I'm trying, but I know it will take time."

"And what about your mom? How is she?"

"Unbelievable. She is one of the toughest women I know. Many of my friends' moms would have probably walked out. I'm sure they told her to. But she wouldn't. Maybe it was wrong. Maybe it was right. I know that there were times I wanted her to. But she knew something that none of us kids knew. She knew what our lives would be like if she left. We were hurting already, and she knew that we would hurt more if she walked out. I can see that now. She knew that my dad could be helped. She believed in medicine and in my dad. She knew that he just hadn't found the right doctor, the right help. And she was right. If my mom hadn't held on, I wouldn't have reconciled with my dad. He would still be the monster I thought he was. Because my mom was strong, she was the glue that kept our family together. And I am so glad she did what she did."

Josie saw a steeliness in her mother that not only saved her and her siblings from the deep pain of divorce, but also likely saved her father from continuing his downward spiral. Though there were some tough times along the way, Josie's mother ultimately gave her the gift of free-dom—freedom from the fear of her family breaking up and from the fear of making future commitments.

Mom as Mentor

Acting as a mentor and being a role model are two different things—though moms do both. When we model behavior to our daughters, it is something we do every day—without thinking about it, and usually without talking about it. Your daughter simply sees the benefits—or detriments—of your behavior, internalizes that behavior, and makes it her own (either in subconscious imitation, which is generally what happens, or in conscious reaction). Kids watch their parents all the time. They want to see what you are doing, why you are doing it, and most importantly of all, they want to know how you perceive *them*. If a mother comes home from work and passes by her daughter without acknowledgment while talking on her phone, the daughter feels unimportant. If this behavior happens repeatedly, she will internalize this feeling and *believe* she is unimportant. If, on the other hand, her mother hangs up her phone and smiles at her daughter as she asks her how her day was, the daughter feels significant and wanted. Always remember that the behavior you model teaches life lessons about personal worth and how to live.

Mentoring, on the other hand, is about consciously, openly teaching daughters about life. Part of it is still teaching by example, but much of it is teaching by discussion or instruction. When medical students and residents follow me around my practice, they can note how I examine my patients, but my fellow doctors and I are also a little like coaches, helping these medical students with questions they have about making a proper diagnosis or prescribing an effective treatment.

Mothers mentor their daughters in ways that most fathers can't. Mothers usually spend more time with their daughters than dads do, and because they are both women, they tend to talk more and discuss their feelings more openly. Women think differently than men do, and this gives mothers an advantage over fathers when it comes to mentoring their daughters because we have a better idea of our how our daughters see the world and think about it.

Julie's mother had graduated from college and worked as a bank teller until she had children. At that point, she became a full-time, stay-at-home mom. Julie was the youngest of three kids, and by the time she was a junior in high school, she was the only child still at home. Her mother decided to go back to school and get another degree. Julie told her mother that she thought it was a great idea, but secretly she feared that her mother would fail miserably. After all, in Julie's mind, her mother was *old*.

Julie's mother took two years of college classes to freshen her learning skills, but she had a bigger plan that she didn't tell her family about yet: she was determined to go to law school. After earning a 4.0 GPA during those two years of college, she felt ready to move forward. She applied to several top law schools and ended up going to the University of Michigan. When she told her husband and Julie, they were stunned, elated, and scared. What had she gotten herself into? She was nearing fifty. Was she really going to be able to keep up with the demanding schedule? The answer was yes. She excelled in law school, graduated, and joined a very good law firm.

When Julie finished college, she thought about law school too. But was torn. Could she excel as her mother had? Could she balance a career and family life? She talked to her mother, who invited her to spend a year working at the firm to see if she liked it. Over that year, she and her mother had great conversations. Her mother encouraged her not to be anxious, not to think too far ahead, and certainly not to feel obligated to follow her into the field of law.

Julie moved into marketing and the business world, but she still felt restless and kept thinking about law school. Her mother told her, "Never make decisions out of fear. If you believe that your heart is telling you to go in one direction, then jump."

So Julie took the plunge and went to law school—and then wondered if she had made a terrible mistake. During her first year, she often called her mother, wanting to quit. "I just can't do it, mom. I'm just not cut out for this. I know that one of these times I'm going to fail—and then I will feel like my life is over. I'm just not you. You are smarter than I am, tougher than I am."

Her mother would listen patiently and then tell Julie to pull herself together and do the best she could. Even if she flunked out of law school, her life would not be over. Being a lawyer was just a job, and she'd had jobs before. It wasn't nearly as important as family and friends.

"Probably the most important lesson my mom taught me," she said, "was to keep my head on my shoulders and my priorities straight. When I did that, then I stopped worrying about my grades and the workload. I really believe that my mother pulled me through law school. And I am so grateful to her."

My own mother mentored me through college, medical school, and my early years as a mother. She was tough, but encouraging. She always reassured me that I could meet challenges and achieve success.

All mothers do this, with greater or lesser success, but no mother is hopeless at being a mentor. Many worry about mistakes that they made in the past. They worry that they have failed their daughters in some way, or irreparably frayed their relationship, or that it is too late to forge a new, healthier relationship with their daughter. This is *not* true. It is *never* too late to restore the bond between a mother and daughter. Asking for and receiving forgiveness is part of life. Daughters will expect mothers to take the lead in reconciling and healing, but they desire it as much as you do.

Being a good mother is perhaps the most humbling experience a woman can have. It begins with looking back at our own childhoods, separating the good from the bad, learning the lessons of our own lives, and consciously employing them to be good mothers. This is a challenge because it is hard to model good parenting if your own childhood was marred by bad, inadequate, absent, or painful parenting. Bad behaviors have a way reproducing themselves. But the thing to remember is that it doesn't have to be that way. You can be a great role model regardless of your upbringing. In fact, you may be a better model because you understand how bad modeling affects children. Make a list. Write down the behaviors you want to avoid and those you want to model. If we keep the plan vague—"I'll just do the best I can to be kind and patient"—we set ourselves up for failure. (And we grandmothers need to make lists too, because sometimes we're prone to giving advice when we shouldn't.)

You can even get more detailed with a list of ideas for when things go wrong. For example, "When I feel like I'm getting angry, I'll excuse myself and come back when my frustration has subsided." You might think this instruction is just for you, but imagine what a great example it is to your daughter! You are modeling how to handle intense emotions with grace and restraint. That's a skill she will absolutely need at school, with friends, and in her future.

Modeling good behavior requires you to take time for self-reflection and take a hard look at how you respond to your daughter. When you do so, don't just focus on the big stuff, because great modeling can come in small, seemingly insignificant ways.

Claire grew up as the only child of a single mother who worked long hours at a bakery. Claire often started her day before school at the bakery and finished her day by doing her homework while her mom worked. I asked her if she found it hard to live this way.

"You know, I never thought much about it," she said. "I certainly didn't feel sorry for myself. It's simply how life was. Sure, I had friends who didn't live this way. But I never heard my mother complain. She was grateful she had a job that she enjoyed and that paid the bills. She showed me that hard work wasn't something to be afraid of. I saw her exhausted at night, but then she'd be up the next morning to do it all over again."

When I spoke with Claire, she had just opened a very successful marketing business—and the key to her success, she told me, was her mother's example of hard work.

Most of the time, we mothers model many good lessons in simple things—sticking with a commitment, speaking well of others without jealousy or spite, showing forgiveness or grace to a friend, and extending kindness. These little examples can loom large for our daughters.

How to Mentor Well

Effective mentoring begins with knowing your daughter's goals—not just for a career, but for life—and providing a roadmap for moral behavior from the time she is in grade school to the time she is a mature woman.

Mentoring takes modeling to a different, more intellectual level. While modeling demonstrates good behavior, mentoring is about discussing *why* the behavior is good. While your own behavior can demonstrate or model self-restraint when it comes to anger, mentoring means helping your daughter deal with her own struggles in controlling her temper by talking them out and giving her strategies to deal with her emotions. One of these strategies might be giving your children an "emotional vocabulary"—assigning words to identify the feelings they experience. Once identified, they are easier to control.

If your daughter bursts into tears because she failed a test or because a friend said something mean to her, have her identify her feelings. (This is usually easier with a daughter than with a son because girls are more prone to discuss their feelings with their moms.) Did she feel shame, did she feel belittled, or did she feel angry with herself or against her friend? Once she knows what the feeling was, you can tell her how to deal with it. Suppose she was angry with herself for failing an exam. She can either berate herself endlessly (which achieves nothing practical) or she can shake it off and vow to do better next time, learning from the experience and applying it to her future studies.

If she is incensed that a friend would say something hurtful to her, you can talk to her about why responding in kind is not the answer because it only degrades herself. You can also explain why the proper course is to ignore the unkind words and recognize that her inherent value does not depend on what her friends or schoolmates think of her.

The skill of understanding her deep feelings and learning to control her reactions to them will be critical to her later success in relationships, school, and work—in fact, just about everything she does in life. That skill will also give her tremendous self-confidence and a sense of freedom because *she* will control her emotions; *they* won't control her.

Since mentoring a daughter is teaching a daughter, take inventory of your interactions with her over the past two weeks. What were your conversations like? Did you do things together? Did you have any disagreements? And if so, how were they resolved?

Fathers often mentor sons through sports or shared hobbies. Mothers often mentor daughters by reading books together. It can start easily by reading to her when she's a young child. Later, you could form a mother-daughter book club where you read and discuss books together and the lessons they might teach. Girls—being more emotionally sensitive, verbal, and communicative than boys—can relish reading novels, especially novels about relationships, and talking about them. Using classic novels can be a great and fulfilling way to help mentor your daughter through examining the examples set by the characters in the story.[2]

Teaching Your Daughter Tenacity

It's easy for most mothers to teach our daughters to go into the world and accomplish great things—to follow their passions, to use their talents, to do well in school, to seek a career, to make money, and to be successful. Our culture supports all of that to a fault because the focus is all on the self. It neglects the far more important quality of altruistic resolve, which is the tenacity women often need to hold their families together. Character counts more than career, and family is more important than fortune. Kids in troubled families know this to be true; mothers should know it too.

That means putting the needs of others before our own. That can be easier said than done—and is, in fact, often said and not done. Self-sacrifice is something that we know is a virtue, but for many it can be a hard one to emulate.

Now to be clear, I am not advocating that mothers ignore their own needs and let their daughters become the center of their lives. That can be harmful. When a child is the center of the home and a mother's life revolves around her, the child feels far too powerful, and that's when kids get "spoiled." Your daughter needs to know that you are in charge. Your self-sacrifice comes not from *indulging* her, but by making familial stability and security your priority and by not letting your house devolve into chaos with everyone pursuing their own selfish interests. Every individual in the family should be willing to do what is necessary for the good of the whole—and mothers often need to take the lead in this.

When Julie was six, she remembers fighting with her older sister. They pulled one another's hair, refused to sleep in the same bedroom, and by all rights appeared to hate one another. This went on through their teen years. Julie's mom was a single mother and they didn't have much money. After school, Julie and her sister went to their aunt's home until their mother returned from work at dinnertime. Even when they were at their aunt's house, they fought. On several occasions, she remembers her aunt yelling at them to stop, insisting that she wouldn't watch them after school if they didn't quit being so mean to each other.

"At the time, that sounded great to me," Julie said. "I thought that going home and having the house all to ourselves when we were ten and eleven would be fantastic." But their aunt thought better of her threat and insisted that they keep coming to her house.

"I can remember, though," Julie said, "how my mother talked to us. She never yelled. Sometimes she cried when she heard us fighting and that made me really sad. I would stay away from my sister for a while because I felt guilty, but we always started up again. The funny thing is, I honestly don't know why we fought so much. I knew I loved my sister and that I needed her. She was a year older and I thought that she would know what to do if something went wrong. As an adult, I look back on those days and just scratch my head. So much time was lost. Fighting now seems so ridiculous.

"But here's the thing that I remember most: every day my mother would come home and ask about our day. She would listen to us complain. Of course, we would argue as we reported to her. When we were finished, she said to us, 'Girls—you know this is bad behavior. You need to show one another love. I'm disappointed in you. Before you go to bed tonight, you need to tell me something you're grateful for.' Or sometimes she would mix it up and make us say something we liked about each other—and boy was that hard. We would say it—but of course with a sneer."

I asked Julie what it was like when she and her sister were older. She told me this story: "One day, my sister decided that she was leaving home. She was seventeen, hated school, and packed her things and left. She left before I got home from school and never told my mother. It was terrifying. We didn't know where she was. My mother called my sister's friends and finally called the police. After about three days we found that she had gone to live with a boyfriend who was twenty-five. I can still remember how hard my mom cried."

But she did more than cry; she learned where the boyfriend lived and went to his apartment. He opened the door, and without a "hello" she walked into the living room and found her daughter Wanda asleep on the couch. She woke her up and Wanda exploded in anger, yelling at her mother and telling her to leave. But her mother sensed that Wanda wasn't herself. Her words were slurred and random, her sentences didn't logically flow or make sense, and she sounded as if she was high on drugs.

She couldn't get Wanda to leave with her, but every Friday she returned to the apartment, and every day for weeks the same scenario unfolded. One Friday, however, she found Wanda alone and unconscious. Her mother called an ambulance. Wanda was in the hospital for five days suffering from a drug overdose, but she survived. Julie visited her every day. They cried together. They apologized to one another.

Wanda went home, and life was different. Julie and Wanda rarely fought. They even got jobs working together at a local department store. One day they received a call at work. It was the emergency department at the local hospital: their mother had suffered a heart attack. Thankfully, she recovered. One evening, she and her daughters were sitting in the living room. Julie began to talk.

"Mom," she began, "you have always been the rock in our family. When we were young brats, you loved us. When we were mean to you because we were angry at life, you loved us. When that guy from church asked you out, you refused to go because you didn't want to take time away from us. When Wanda ran away, you followed her. When we were young, you always made us say something nice about each other or tell you what we were grateful for. Thank you, Mom. You held us together. You taught us how and why to be committed to one another. I can't imagine having a better mom than you."

Julie's mother did what she did because she knew it was right and because she realized that if she didn't hold the family together, it would fall apart. And with all of her might, she decided that she wasn't going to let that happen.

Did she make a lot of mistakes? Of course. But after hearing Julie's story, I am convinced that mothers like hers have a lot to teach us about how to raise strong daughters.

Of course it's never easy, and success is not guaranteed. Every mother (including me) receives "the list" when her kids reach their mid-twenties or early thirties. This is when our grown children inform us of the mistakes we made and how it affected them. Some mothers' lists are short, and others' lists are so long they are too painful to talk about. The truth is that we all fail at modeling many things. We miss hundreds of opportunities to mentor our daughters in the areas that we want to. And as much as we all long to keep our families intact, sometimes with the best efforts we put forth, we still fail.

Many mothers and daughters have volatile relationships. I have seen thousands of girls grow up—and I've often foreseen looming conflicts with their mothers. The mothers facing these conflicts often fit a pattern or a type.

- **Needy Mothers.** These are the mothers who believe they must be their child's everything: cook, counselor, coach, teacher, ever-present friend, room mom, girl scout leader, and friend to her daughter's friends. Now these things by themselves can be laudable. But when a mother thinks that her daughter can't (or won't) live a good life without her constant involvement, she is overdoing it and headed for trouble. Daughters who live at home when they are twenty-six because they can't find a job are often victims of mothers who need to be needed. Some of these daughters assume they need to stay at home to keep their mothers "happy," and that's when you have obvious cases of codependency.

- **Controlling Mothers.** These mothers are the bossy ones. They pick out their daughters' clothes, friends, and activities and tell them what to do with their time at home. They don't mentor their daughters; they dominate them. Some mothers do this out of fear, believing that they must always be in control or terrible things will happen. Others were raised by controlling mothers and repeat what they know. Still others are reacting against the unhappiness of their own childhoods and want to rigidly organize their daughters' lives to avoid the mistakes of their own. A controlling mother implies, "I know who you are, and you don't." She sees herself as the custodian and controller of her child's mind. Having been told repeatedly that mother knows best, children of controlling parents can doubt themselves, and even simple, independent decisions can fill them with anxiety. They also learn to lie—to say what the controlling mother wants to hear—in order to keep her happy.

- **The Distant Mother.** Distant mothers rarely show affection for their daughters and rarely have sincere and deep conversations with them. Sometimes they are simply socially awkward—even with their own family—or they grew up in an environment where they received little affection. Daughters who grow up with distant mothers often feel unworthy; they take their mothers' lack of affection personally and believe that their mothers fail to show them love, empathy, or compassion because there is something wrong with them and they deserve to be emotionally abandoned. This, needless to say, can be a serious problem, and a mother's prolonged emotional absence has even been shown to affect the physical and chemical make-up of a child's brain.[3]

- **Best Friend Mothers.** Every loving mother wants to be close to her daughter. When my mother passed away, I lost one of my best friends. Desiring an intimate relationship with a daughter where you share your deepest wishes and fears is a longing in the hearts of both mothers and daughters. Mothers often assume that being a daughter's best friend is beneficial for both parties, but that's not always true. There is a serious difference between being a parent and being your daughter's best friend, and it is terribly harmful to your daughter if you mix up those roles. The time to transition from being a parent to a friend should occur when your daughter is in her twenties and living on her own. When your daughter is young—including when she's in high school—she needs the security of you being the grown up—the authority who can guide her and protect her. When a mother acts as a daughter's best friend, she inevitably has problems with discipline. In that case, the relationship is more like that of one sibling to another, which leads the daughter to lose confidence in her mother. When she loses confidence, she fails to feel safe. She doesn't feel that she can trust her mother to make good judgments, give healthy rules, and give her the guidance she desperately wants. When a teen lives with a mother acting as her best friend, she can feel as though her mother is competing with her in a sort of sibling rivalry. Mothers who boast that they can "wear their daughter's jeans" communicate to their daughters that they are just like them, and their daughters often feel shortchanged in the comparison. A healthy mother allows her daughter to have her own day.

Moms, if you are going to wear jeans, wear "mom jeans." And if that makes you feel dowdy, then wear tight jeans out with your husband—not when you pick your daughter up at school. Daughters don't want their mothers to be their best friends until they are older. As one teen girl once told me several years ago, "Dr. Meeker, when my mom is around my friends, trying to buddy up to them, it just feels creepy. I mean I love her and all, but I don't want her in my circle of friends." I get it. When my teen daughters were home with friends, I was often tempted to jump into the middle of a conversation. But it's important to let our daughters navigate their friendships on their own. If your daughter needs advice, then she'll seek it. She's more likely to seek it from you if she respects you as someone older and more mature than her friends—and not just another one of her pals.

Once your daughter has become an adult, it's fine to dive in as a friend; at that stage in her life, it's an affirmation of her own adulthood. You can be best friends because you no longer need to discipline her, give her tough guidance, or be her authority figure. Think about it. If you wait a mere twenty years and act as a good parent, you can then be best friends with your daughter for decades to come. But if you insist on being her best friend when she is a child and even a teen, your future relationship will suffer. She will lack respect for you and won't confide in you. She won't see you as a model or a mentor because you insisted on being an equal. And she certainly won't see you as the backbone of the family because that's the role of a grown-up.

Now having read all this—even if you see some bad traits in yourself—take heart. Most mothers fall prey to some of these shortcomings at some time or another. I know I have. I have tried to control my kids, sidled up to their teen friends, and occasionally made other mistakes—maybe too many to mention. The trick is to recognize when you've made a mistake and stop doing it. We all make mistakes—and most of us feel the nagging of conscience or intuition that tells us we should stop. Listen to that intuition, that voice of conscience, and remember that the best three things we can be to our daughters are a role model, a mentor, and the glue that holds the family together. And be assured that these are what every daughter longs for in her mother.

Chapter Four

Dads: Be Her First Love, Protector, and Leader

On Christmas morning in 1986, I found a large box wrapped in simple paper under our Christmas tree. Our family was small back then with only my husband, Walt, our one-year-old daughter, and myself. I knew the gift was from Walt, and I immediately felt embarrassed. He had gone out and bought me something lovely, and I hadn't done the same for him. We were living in Milwaukee, where I was doing my pediatric residency at a large children's hospital. My work hours were grueling and time for shopping was limited. The time I spent at work made me feel even more guilty on this Christmas morning. Walt and I had agreed the year before that he would stay home with our young daughter for the three years of my residency, and then he would do his residency after I finished. The arrangement worked well for us, but I can't honestly say I felt good about it most of the time. I loved my work, but I desperately wanted to be home with our small family.

That Christmas was a sweet one. It wasn't just the large box that made me feel loved; it was the sacrifice Walt had made for me to finish my pediatric medical training. That was almost thirty-three years ago, and I still feel grateful. When I opened the box, I found a lovely blue boiled wool coat with a beautiful, matching silk lining. And—because it was the 1980s—it had shoulder pads that were just big enough. We endured freezing winters in Milwaukee, and he knew that I complained constantly about being cold. Hence the extra-warm coat.

The coat fit perfectly, and I wore it everywhere. About a month after Christmas, we boarded a plane for Boston to visit my family. While sitting on the plane, I noticed that the buttons were a bit small for the buttonholes, and I thought this was a little peculiar for such a nice coat. I leaned over to Walt and said, "Where did you get this? The buttons are a bit small."

At first, he pretended not to hear me, so I repeated myself. Finally, he said, "I made the coat for you."

Wham bam. I felt terrible for criticizing the buttons, almost burst into tears for his act of kindness, and was frankly stunned. I felt so well-loved, and I felt I didn't deserve it. How in the world did he know how to sew such a magnificent coat? I knew only enough about sewing to know that boiled wool is a very expensive fabric.

But for Walt, sewing soon became a passion. He made a red and black checked coat for our one-year-old, and when our second daughter was born, he made a white and black checked one for her, as well. The three of us stayed very warm during those long, frigid Milwaukee winters.

As the girls grew, they knew that their dad made their coats, and they wore them as proudly as I wore mine. When the girls outgrew them, our third and fourth children wore them. The wool coats were indestructible. Eventually, of course, all four kids outgrew their coats. Our children moved on to high school and then college, but they kept their coats in our front hall closet. They showed them to their friends; they were proud of them.

After our second daughter graduated from college, she decided to go to Indonesia to teach. After a few months, she became homesick and called home to ask her dad a special favor: "Can you make me another coat—like the one you made me when I was little?"

So Walt trekked down to our local fabric store, bought white and black checked fabric, and out came his sewing machine. Within a few weeks, the coat was done. My adult daughter wore that coat as if it were a lifesaver. It connected her to her dad who was half a world away.

I have often said that a father is the most important man in a daughter's life, and the older I get, the truer that statement becomes to me. I have seen literally thousands of girls grow up—and whether their fathers doted on them or were workaholics, were single fathers or absent fathers, were financially successful or in jail—in every case they remained the most important men in their daughters' lives. Here's why.

Inevitably, every father sets the template for how his daughter thinks about men. If her father was kind, she will trust men. If her father was affectionate, she will expect other men to be affectionate. If her father was distant or cruel, she will expect other men to be the same—and this can have consequences even larger than one might realize. I have spoken with adult women who have a hard time believing in God because their personal experiences made it difficult for them to believe in a loving Father. A daughter's experience with her earthly father affects every relationship she will have with every male figure in her life. And I am convinced that if every father could see himself through his daughter's eyes for just fifteen minutes, his life would never be the same.

Girls who securely attach to their fathers when they are young grow up to be more self-assured. And when they are more self-confident, they have healthier relationships with men. Teen girls who are strongly bonded to their fathers are far less likely to become sexually active or pregnant, or to seek relationships with selfish, cruel, or disrespectful boys. And what does it take to be a good father like this? It really means just showing up, being there, and being the sort of father that you want to be—and that your daughter needs you to be.

Dad as First Love

Typically when I ask a mother about her relationship with her daughter, she'll say something like, "Oh, it's great. We are very close and are good friends." If I ask a dad, he'll look puzzled and fall back on listing his daughter's achievements. If I ask their daughters, though, the answers I get are immediate and clear. "Oh, my dad is great. He is always offering to help with homework or asking how my friends are. He loves to do things with me, and my mom usually doesn't like the stuff we do. She thinks it's dangerous."

Or I may get a response like, "I don't know. I never see my dad. I miss him. Ever since he and my mom divorced, we've just grown apart. We don't talk much, and I think he's just gotten busy with his new life." In these cases, I hear despair in their voices. The love they want and need from their dads feels gone—and when he's not there, they sometimes imagine their own version of him.

Recently, I spoke to a twelve-year-old girl whose father was in prison. Her single mother moved out of state to find work, leaving this young girl with her grandmother. She was close to her grandmother but missed her parents terribly. She wanted to be back with her mother, but what struck me was what she said about her father: "My dad's getting out of prison soon, you know. I can't wait, because when he does, I'm going to go live with him. I'm special to my dad, and I know that when we are together, life is going to be so much better."

She craved her father's love, no matter his circumstances. He loved her as no one else could, and she thought of him as her hero. In fact, her father was not the good man she described to me, but in his absence she imagined the man she desperately wanted and needed—and that was both heartbreaking and inspiring. I've seen similar reactions from daughters many times. Every father is his daughter's first love. I know that many fathers don't like to hear this because they consider it a heavy burden, but a father will always be the most important man in his daughter's life.

Dad as Protector

Daughters feel more secure and loved when their fathers watch out for them. When a father shows that he is willing to fight for and protect his daughter, she wears it as a badge of honor.

When I was sixteen, a boyfriend (a very nice guy) took me to a movie that was highly inappropriate. It was filled with sex, foul language—you name it. He was naïve, and neither of us had any idea what the movie was about when we bought tickets. When he brought me home, my father met us and asked what movie we saw. When he heard the name, he immediately demanded that my boyfriend leave. I was mortified. I yelled at my dad. I don't think that I spoke with him for several days. Later, I came to appreciate what my father had done—and to respect him even more for it.

He showed me he was willing to protect me. While I was very upset at first, I soon realized that he acted as he did because he loved me. Of course, I would never admit that to my dad until many years later, but in seeing him protect me, I learned something about protecting myself. My mother felt the same way my father did about the movie, but she was too nice and polite to make a scene with my boyfriend. Dad acted on the spot.

In doing so, my father showed me how to be assertive. It's one thing for a father to tell his daughter about asserting herself. It's another thing for him to show her. I heard his voice, felt the awkwardness, and saw my father plow through. I eventually realized that while assertiveness can be uncomfortable and can offend another person, it is sometimes necessary to protect the people we love. My boyfriend certainly was offended (and forever afraid of my dad), but I learned that his discomfort was okay, because ultimately my dad was right. Dads protect their daughters in part by setting boundaries for them; no one can do that better. And when a dad sets the boundaries, he teaches his daughter to respect herself and demand better behavior from boys, and eventually men. Sadly, many girls grow up never seeing a father (or mother) set high standards for them because parents too often believe they are being intrusive and need to let their daughters make their own decisions. But you will help her make better decisions if you set the rules—and she wants you to do that.

Even as early as elementary school, girls are pressured to be "sexy." Once girls hit size seven (in first or second grade), the racks of scant, inappropriate clothing targeting children explode. It gets even worse as the girls get older, and one of the biggest areas of contention between teen daughters and parents is over clothes. Parents are torn. On the one hand, parents (mostly mothers) want their daughters to fit in with the girls in their class. Fathers, on the other hand, often feel protective of their young daughters and insist that they wear more modest clothes. Daughters get upset, and frequently mothers intervene, insisting to their husbands that they don't understand current fashion. This is the way all girls dress, they say, and many fathers at this point recede into the background and question their instincts.

I tell fathers, please don't. Fathers understand how boys look at girls, and they don't want their daughter viewed this way; they don't want their daughter regarded as a sex object rather than as an intelligent, capable young woman. And they don't want their daughters to think of themselves as sex objects.

Dads are right. Girls who dress in "sexy" clothes are focused too heavily on their sexuality and are far more likely to engage in sexual activity, which can be enormously harmful to their mental, physical, and emotional health. My advice to fathers is to trust your protective instincts and intervene. You do your daughter a favor when you teach her that who she is—her personality and character—is far more important than how "sexy" she is.

We know that daughters whose fathers are present in their lives have higher cognitive and linguistic development; score higher on achievement tests; have higher IQ scores; show better academic and school performance (including behavior); are more self-reliant, self-directed, and self-confident; have higher levels of sociability and self-control; are far less likely as teens to be depressed, sexually active, or involved with drugs (all three tend to go together); are more successful in their professional lives; and have happier marriages. The benefits to a daughter of having a dad around the house are acute.[1]

A father has such a profound effect on his daughter's life because he is central to the formation of her own identity. The value a father places on his daughter will, to a large degree, influence the value she places on herself. A father who is extremely critical of his daughter can leave her feeling unworthy, even as an adult. A loving father who accepts and approves of his daughter teaches her to believe in and like herself. A father who abandons his family leaves a daughter with a sense of insecurity and an unfulfilled desire for masculine affirmation and attention (that can come from dangerous sources otherwise).

Daughters are exceptionally sensitive to their fathers' behavior—to what they say and do. Daughters desperately want to be loved and accepted. Many of them see their fathers as larger-than-life figures, and winning their approval is a life goal. A father's demeanor can affect his daughter's behavior. If a father wants his daughter to have patience, there is no greater way to influence her than to show her what patience looks like. I have spoken with countless women who have said that they are successful in their personal and professional lives because of the way their fathers lived. Their fathers gave them a living model of strong character.

Many years ago, I came home from work to meet four hungry kids and an empty refrigerator. I picked up the phone and ordered Chinese takeout. My husband offered to pick it up (I think because the kids and I were all getting testy because of hunger). As he was walking out the door, I shouted, "Whatever you do, don't forget the egg rolls!" (I love egg rolls.) At the last minute, my eight-year-old daughter asked if she could go with him. He said sure.

They returned about thirty minutes later. I opened the bags, pulled out the white cardboard boxes, and sighed with disgust. "I knew it!" I said. "I just knew that you'd forget the egg rolls. You're always forgetting things." I ranted on, citing examples, until my eight-year-old daughter came up and yanked my shirt to get my attention.

"Mom," she whispered, "don't be mad at Dad."

"Why not?"

"On our way home from the restaurant, we saw a man going through a trash can. Dad pulled over and offered him our Chinese food."

Inevitably, the homeless man didn't take the chicken stir fry or the beef and rice; he took my egg rolls.

But in that moment, I suddenly realized how selfish and unfair I had been. I apologized to my husband.

But the really important thing is the effect my husband's example had on my daughter. When she graduated from college, she decided to forgo a well-paying teaching job in the States in order to do teaching and missionary work among the poor in Indonesia.

Today she is thirty-three and is one of the humblest women I have ever known. She values others regardless of their age or socioeconomic status. She respects them and loves them. She does this because her father taught her the virtue of humility. He taught her that every man, woman, and child is of equal value. And she learned this one way—by watching her dad live it before her eyes.

Fathers lead their daughters every day by example. As a dad, I'm sure that's hard to hear. It can feel intimidating and overwhelming knowing that someone who admires and needs you watches your every move. But that's the reality. Your daughter is always noting your attitudes, behaviors, and actions and adopting many of them as her own—and they might not always be the ones you want.

I remember one father approached me after a conference and said, "Dr. Meeker, can I ask your opinion about something?"

"Of course."

"My ex-wife and I are having an argument. You see, I was in jail for a couple of years and I just got out. I'm doing really well now and want to reestablish a relationship with my nine-year-old daughter. She's hesitant, and I get it. I haven't exactly been a good example. And between the divorce and my years in jail, my daughter doesn't know me very well. And, Dr. Meeker, here's the problem: my ex-wife visited me only once when I was in prison—and when she did, she took a picture of me in my orange jump suit. She taped that photo onto the refrigerator so that my daughter saw it every day. She wants my daughter to learn from my mistakes. But that's what I've been reduced to—a mistake."

"You should insist that your ex-wife take that picture down," I said. "You shouldn't be shamed—especially when you're turning your life around—and that shaming isn't doing your daughter any good. Your ex-wife needs to understand that your daughter will look up to you, regardless of your mistakes, because you are her father. And if she doesn't see you and admire you for the man you are now, she will be more—not less—likely to emulate your mistakes."

Many parents wrongly assume that they should tell their kids about their own mistakes as a warning not to do as they did. Unfortunately, this rarely works. In fact, it can have the opposite effect. A child or teen will feel more confident that the bad behavior her parents confessed to won't hurt her either.

A Father's Dedication

Many fathers have heart-breaking problems with their teen daughters. One gentleman recently told me, "I've lost her. We used to be so close. Not anymore. I try to hug her, and she gets stiff as a board and makes me feel like I am the most disgusting person on the planet. I just don't know what to do."

I asked him whether his daughter had changed friends, or had suffered some trauma, or was taking drugs.

"Oh, I'm sure she's not using drugs. There's no trauma that I know of, and her friends are pretty much the same, and they're still nice to me."

We talked a bit more, and I told him what I thought was going on. "The teen years can be brutal for girls," I said. "Hormones make their moods fluctuate wildly. Most girls feel extremely insecure about their looks, their abilities—you name it. Your daughter is probably doubting herself, wondering whether anyone really likes her, trying to figure out where she fits in, comparing herself to others, and feeling terrible. Her internal angst spills over onto you, but it's not about you, and it's crucial that you shouldn't take it personally."

Many fathers in similar situations simply retreat from their daughters. But this is the worst thing fathers can do. Research shows that when fathers stay involved with their teen daughters, the girls benefit tremendously. It is your best method for limiting emotional and behavioral problems—or getting through them faster. You are her best shield against every danger she will face in her teen years.[2]

Remember that most fathers go through a period of feeling estranged from their daughters. This is entirely normal and is part of your daughter's process of growing up. Just as mothers need to allow their sons to separate from them during the teen years, a similar but less dramatic event happens with daughters and their fathers. If you are a dad who is experiencing behavior changes in your daughter and feels like she is pulling away from you, here are some things you can do.

First, ask yourself the questions I asked the troubled father about whether his daughter had changed friends, or suffered some sort of trauma, or started using drugs. These dangers are usually *not* the problem, but just make sure. Second, remember that you are the leader. Regardless of how she acts, she wants you to be the leader. This means that you need to take the lead in continuing to show affection. If your daughter rebuffs your overtures, try to show your affection in a different way. Instead of giving her a bear-hug in public, pat her unobtrusively on the shoulder, or pull up a chair by her bed and try talking with her before she goes to sleep—maybe even hold her hand. Ask how her day was. It doesn't matter whether the conversation is long or short, whether she participates eagerly or mumbles just a few words. It's the effort that counts. When you do errands on the weekends, ask her to go with you. Or take her to breakfast. The key thing is to leave her in no doubt that you are always thinking about her, that you want to hear what she has to say, that you enjoy her company, and that you love her regardless of the emotional turmoil she's going through or the bad behavior that represents it.

Whatever you do, *never* give up, because no matter how she behaves, your daughter wants a better relationship with you. She wants you to help her figure out life, but most teens don't know how to ask. That's why you must take the lead, that's why you must never give up, and that's why you must do everything you can to stay engaged in your daughter's life.

Emily's parents divorced when she was twelve. An only child, she spent most weekdays with her mother and most weekends with her father. She showed no serious behavioral problems until her sophomore year of high school, when she became argumentative and started dressing in provocative clothes. Her mother had started dating, and Emily, like many teens of divorced parents, didn't want her mother's boyfriend around. He didn't belong in their family, she said, and she resented the time her mother spent away from her and with him.

Emily told me, "I just wanted to leave my mom's house. I didn't like her boyfriend, and when my mom got mad at me, I snapped."

She was struggling with latent grief over her parents' divorce. "I just felt like I didn't fit anywhere. No place felt like home anymore."

Emily felt "mad and confused" and began hanging out with a new set of kids—the type "parents don't want you to be with."

She admitted to me that she wanted her parents' attention. "I started spending more time at my dad's. He didn't have a girlfriend, and I felt safer there. I don't know why—I just did. My dad worked a lot, and that was hard, but I think he kind of felt sorry for me. I didn't really know my dad that well before the divorce, and I was sort of anxious when I first started hanging out at his house. I didn't know how he'd respond. And I was surprised that he seemed to like having me around—even when I was mad or acted obnoxious. It was like he could handle it. When he came home, we ate dinner together, even though we didn't talk much. He'd ask me a few questions about school, and I sort of ignored him. But because he asked night after night, I started thinking that maybe he really wanted to know. So I started opening up, and the more I started talking to him, the more he seemed interested in listening. I mean, I'm sure he was bored, but he didn't act like it. Then one night, he asked me if I wanted to go out to dinner. I thought it was weird to go to dinner alone with my dad, but I went. At first it was kind of awkward, but after a while, it was kind of fun.

"After that, I got more comfortable with my dad. We always did something together on the weekends. Usually they were little things, like taking the dog for a walk, or going to a movie, or visiting a relative."

As Emily spoke, her demeanor changed. She became brighter. She sat more upright. "The cool thing was that even though my dad isn't a big talker, he did ask how I was handling his and mom's divorce. I couldn't believe it. No one had asked that before. I didn't know what to say, so I just told him that I hated it. I hated that he and my mom weren't together. I hated that I had to go back and forth. I hated that my mom had a boyfriend. All this bad stuff just came pouring out. My dad didn't get mad; he just listened. I spend a lot of time with my father now because he gets me, and I know he wants to be with me—and that's a great feeling. It helped me get through a difficult time."

Mothers know that they are important in their children's lives because our culture makes a point of celebrating motherhood. But I believe that most fathers don't know how huge they are in their daughters' lives. No father is perfect. Every father messes up. But every dad is a giant to his daughter, and every daughter is the most forgiving person he will ever know because she needs him more than she needs anyone else. What a daughter cares most about is seeing that her father is trying to be a good dad to her. You are her first love, and every kindness you extend to her—every time you wipe away a tear, or listen to her, or acknowledge her as important to you—you are strengthening her sense of self. And she will never forget you or your example.

Chapter Five

Help Her Take Control of Screens

At eleven thirty in the evening, seventeen-year-old Evie heard a loud thumping on her front door. She knew who it was—and it scared her.

When she opened the door, two police officers charged past her and frantically searched the house, starting upstairs.

Five teen boys in the downstairs family room ran out the back door. Four girls stayed behind with Evie. Two policemen came downstairs. One said, "Where are they?"

"Where are who?"

"Come on, young lady. You know who I mean. There are minors with alcohol on the premises. That's illegal. Your neighbors called, said they heard a commotion, and told us that underage drinking was going on. So, I'll ask you one more time. Where are they?"

Evie was frightened, and she didn't want to lie—or get arrested. "Sir, they left. There were five guys. I don't even know who they were. They brought over vodka and beer, and some of us drank it."

"Well then, young lady, everyone here gets a breath test. And since this is your house, you're going first."

Evie was certainly not drunk or even tipsy, but she had an anxious, nervous feeling in the pit of her stomach. When the officer asked where her parents were, she looked away and quietly said, "I'm not sure, sir. They don't know I'm here. I was supposed to be at a friend's house for the weekend. They left Friday and won't be back until Sunday."

"Do they have cell phones?"

"Yes, but please don't call them. I will."

"Okay, you do that. Since this is your home, you are the one responsible. I'm writing you up a citation. Now it's late, so I want you and your friends to stay here. We'll check on you in the morning. Got it?"

"Yes, sir." When Evie shut the door, she and her friends were shaking, too afraid to even talk. They had never been in trouble before, and now they had done something so bad that it involved the police.

Evie's parents knew their daughter was a good kid. She got good grades, was polite, obedient, and always wanted to please others. Her teachers loved her. Friends looked up to her. Boys respected her. So they weren't overly worried about going away for a weekend. They had arranged for Evie to stay with a friend whose parents were going to be home so there would be adult supervision, and everything should have been fine.

So what happened? Social media intervened. Evie and her friend decided to go watch a movie at Evie's house and announced that decision on Instagram. Two other girlfriends decided to join them. One of them texted a boy, a senior from another school, and invited him over. He brought three friends with him. When they discovered there were no parents at home, they asked another boy to bring beer and vodka. Evie was mortified, and finally slammed the door on more uninvited guests. They, in turn, called the police out of spite and said minors were drinking at Evie's home. Evie thought she had done nothing wrong—yet everything had gone wrong. Social media can do that to kids; they have no idea how harmful it can be to broadcast every aspect of your life—to constantly update where you're going and what you're doing. Evie learned a tough lesson, but luckily she suffered no serious emotional harm.

A Parent's Deepest Fears

I was one of the lucky parents whose kids got through high school without a cell phone. Yes, those days once existed. If you grew up then—before cell phones and social media—you know that "media" were things you looked at or listened to *occasionally*. No one was *constantly* online or connected to their radio, television, or landline. In retrospect, that gave us some perspective, some calm; we spent most of our time in the real, tangible world, and we weren't bombarded with an endless stream of information and electronic stimulation. Today's kids, however, have their auditory and visual senses overloaded daily, and many people (not just kids) are now obsessed or addicted to laptop movies, email, social media, and video games—sometimes doing several of these things at once, and even feeling fidgety when *not* fidgeting with their phones. As parents, we can sense that this is not good for our kids—that technology is driving a wedge between us, that screens are taking over our children's lives.

The number one fear parents used to express to me was protecting their teenagers from sex, drugs, and alcohol. Now the number one worry is how to protect kids from social media. Parents feel helpless. They believe that social media usage is harming their children and isolating them from normal, healthy relationships and family interactions—and they're right. But they shouldn't feel helpless. Granted, in the past, if you were worried (as you should have been) about raunchy content in movies and vulgarity on television, it was relatively easy to avoid it or keep it switched off. In our new, interconnected age, it is not so easy because the content has gotten in many cases far worse (hardcore pornography has been effectively mainstreamed), and social media platforms have wormed their insidious and addictive ways into too many young girls' hearts.

Parents' fears are justified. But too often they underestimate their influence over their daughters and what they can do to protect them. Let's start by looking at the threat—and why girls are attracted to social media.

Understanding the Danger

Usually when girls first look at Instagram, Facebook, and Snapchat, they do so innocently as wonderful opportunities to express themselves and measure their popularity (beauty, intelligence, and likeability) compared to that of other girls. It is a way to interact with friends (and—warning for parents—strangers). They look forward to receiving comments on their posts and see these as useful guides to fashion—like clothing and makeup—that can enhance their self-image (or actually harm it).

Girls long for approval, and social media platforms offer a way to find it. If others (friends, family, and even strangers) like them, then they can like themselves. Once girls feel accepted and are "liked" enough times, then they believe they have value. But that works only up to a point, because screen approval is not only shallow, but is also short-lived. No matter how much a girl might be praised for being beautiful, sexy, or accomplished, someone will always come along to destroy that view—to criticize, to say something mean, to belittle. Just as positive comments and "likes" bring her joy, negative comments can be devastating to the point that we now talk about "cyberbullying" as a common occurrence and danger.

All teen girls compare themselves to others and have deep-seated insecurities. In more than thirty years of practicing pediatrics, I have never met an exception to this rule. As parents, we may see our daughters as beautiful, smart, and accomplished, but they don't. They see the opposite—they see themselves as falling short of other girls who are prettier, smarter, or more successful.

Because of this normal insecurity, girls are drawn to see how they stack up to others—and social media platforms provide that venue. They offer girls a way to seek acceptance and approval from their peers, but social media usage also leaves them very vulnerable. Here are some of the risks.

Social Media Usage Is Clearly Connected to Depression in Girls

Studies have clearly shown a link between social media usage and depression in girls—and the more a girl is on social media, the higher the risk becomes.[1] That's significant because for many girls, social media platforms become an obsession, a twenty-four-hour notice board of admiration and affirmation—or of criticism and abuse. High usage of social media is linked to poor sleep patterns, bad body image, and low self-esteem—not to mention vulnerability to online harassment.

In a landmark study, researcher Melissa Hunt and her colleagues from the University of Pennsylvania studied the effect of lowering social media usage among girls. They found a clear correlation between decreased depression in girls with less social media usage. It is important for parents to understand that this link is real. The good news is that when we help our daughters reduce social media usage to about thirty minutes per day, their risk for depression decreases remarkably.[2]

It's not just teens who are vulnerable either. I'll be honest. As a middle-aged woman who has pretty good self-confidence, I stopped looking at Facebook because no matter how good I felt about myself before I went online, once I began looking at what my friends were doing on Facebook, I ended up feeling that I was a loser, that my life was boring, and that my friends were getting more attractive as I was getting older! I couldn't help but wonder what was wrong with me. (What was wrong with me, of course, was that I took these pictures and posts at face-value, rather than as the carefully organized, best-foot-forward self-advertisements that they were.) But if a happy, successful, and secure middle-aged woman could, for no good reason, feel down in the dumps after a quick dip into social media, imagine how depressed a naturally insecure teenage girl might feel after flipping through posts from girls her age wearing the most popular fashions and exquisite make-up with handsome boyfriends hanging off their arms. The answer is that they feel like I initially did while looking at my friends on Facebook—only twenty-nine times more so!

Even if girls know that social media posts are a way for some girls to show off, it doesn't matter. They hold their own value in the balance, and when a girl feels she's constantly coming up short in comparison to others, or experiences repeated rejection, she begins to change her public image. She assumes that she needs to be sexier and skinnier and more fashionable (whatever the fashion happens to be) to be liked.

Adolescent girls are unsure about themselves and are more than willing to adopt different personas in order to be more popular. They want to be mature, they want to be cool, and they often equate sophistication with being sexually provocative. Many parents are shocked by what their daughters do or say on social media—but they often never see the worst of it, because hidden accounts are easy to create.

Christie was a junior in high school, a straight-A student involved in choir and local service work, as well as the oldest of five kids. She never gave her parents a hard time. But then Christie's mother was accosted by the mother of one of Christie's best friends, Sophie.

"I hate to bring this up, but I found some horrible stuff on Sophie's Snapchat," she said. "Sophie posted nude photos of herself—and so did Christie."

"That can't be true!"

"It is. I got into the girls' accounts. It's all there."

Christie's mother, Alicia, felt nauseated. When she picked Christie up from school that day, they drove home in a silent car.

Christie knew something was up, but it wasn't until they pulled into the driveway that her mother began sobbing.

"Mom, what's wrong?"

"Christie, I need you to be honest with me."

Christie was terrified. Suddenly she knew.

"Sophie's mom said you posted a nude photo of yourself on Snapchat. Is that true?"

The look on Christie's fact told her it was.

"Why did you do it, Christie?"

Christie was embarrassed, ashamed, and confused, and she didn't know what to say. So she made the usual teenager's excuse. "Mom, everyone does it; it's no big deal. Some boys asked me to do it, and I kept saying no, until this one guy asked me, and I liked him, and so I did it, and I'm sorry. I don't know what I was thinking. But he mocked me, called me a prude, and said if I didn't post a nude photo like everyone else, he'd tell everyone I was a geek."

"So you were bullied into it?"

"Well—yes. But really, Mom, it's nothing. Even Sophie's done it. On Snapchat pictures go away almost immediately, so there's nothing to worry about."

But there was. Photos from Snapchat *can* be recovered, and some kids take pictures of photos when they appear so they can post them anywhere. Because of their cognitive immaturity, most teens don't realize that what they post now could come back to haunt them.

"I knew this wasn't me," Christie told her mom, "and I guess I know it was wrong and that a real friend wouldn't have asked me to do it, but it felt kind of freeing at the same time to be like everybody else, to fit in, and to be popular. But I won't do it again, because really I don't think it did make me more popular. Actually, I felt used—and I'm sorry."

Alicia grounded Christie for a month. She took away her phone and made her come home from school immediately after choir practice. Christie did as she was told without complaint.

Several weeks later, Sophie told Christie that boys were spreading rumors about her in class. They said she was a "slut" beneath her "Goody Two-shoes" exterior—and her nude Snapchat picture was offered as evidence.

Christie confronted the boys publicly. She called them liars—and they laughed at her. And they started spreading new, more explicit rumors about her—that she was a slut who gave boys oral sex.

Alicia didn't know about these rumors, but she did notice that Christie started complaining about school. Then she dropped out of choir. Her grades fell, she spent more time alone in her room, she didn't go out with her friends, and she was sullen and uncommunicative with her parents.

A counselor told Alicia not to worry. Christie's experience was not unusual, and she felt confident that Christie would come out of her slump.

But she didn't. She never got an A again. She barely finished high school, scraping by in her senior year with Ds and a few Fs. Christie had once hoped to go to an Ivy League School; now she refused to apply to college at all. Christie fell into a severe depression. She told a counselor that she intended to commit suicide. That led to her swift admission into a hospital and treatment for clinical depression.

Fortunately, Christie did eventually recover. But it took years, and many girls aren't so lucky because sex-shaming—like what Christie had endured—is soul-wrenching for young women. Don't let anyone tell you that young women *want* to be or *choose* to be regarded as sexual objects. Women who get caught in this trap of posting provocative social media photos of themselves do so initially because they want attention, popularity, and affirmation that they are attractive. But every girl and every woman wants to believe that she was made for some deep purpose; she craves deeper human relationships. That should be obvious, but screen time emphasizes the superficial. Teens intuit that they are valued for their looks and their sexiness, and they think that posting photos to highlight these things is perfectly acceptable—until they find out the inevitable costs. Putting morality aside, which too many in our society have done, any pediatrician or psychologist can tell you that girls who allow themselves to be treated as sexual objects are at a far higher risk of clinical depression—and the results can be devastating.

Journalist Nancy Jo Sales has written extensively about the harmful effects of social media on girls. She interviewed more than two hundred young women for her book *American Girls: Social Media and the Secret Lives of Teenagers.*[3] She notes that human beings have "evolved to communicate face-to-face." When we communicate with each other, our communication involves not just the words we say, but also our body language. But as kids spend more time on screens, they spend less time on actual face-to-face conversations with people and have a harder time making eye contact and having normal conversations. This makes it easier for boys to view girls as things, as sex objects, rather than as fully fledged people.

To be honest, many parents sound like teenagers when they try to justify their daughters' social media usage. They'll say that "every girl does it" and that it is "harmless because they just text friends." To those parents, I say this: let Christie's story stay in your mind. We shouldn't be naïve about how lovely, innocent girls can be led to do dangerous things they would never otherwise have done because of social media. Their lives can be ruined as a result.

Several years ago, I spoke at a conference for parents and discussed the dangers that arise when girls post nude photos. To my dismay, *most* of the parents—and this was an affluent, well-educated group with daughters an average age of ten years old—believed that posting nude photos "was just a normal thing that that most girls will eventually do." One dad volunteered, "I told my daughter that if she ever posts a nude photo of herself, she should make sure not to show her face. That way, she can stay anonymous."

I was flabbergasted and replied, "Why is her face more important than her body?"

"It isn't. It's just that no one will recognize her."

I warned him that social media wasn't nearly as anonymous as he apparently thought it was and that he was de facto endorsing his daughter's involvement in pornography. The result would be to crush her self-esteem and set her up for sexual abuse. Those were harsh words, I know, but they were true—and I was shocked at how he took it for granted that it was okay for his daughter to dabble in pornography. But pornography is a big part of the problem. It has dulled many of our standards of right and wrong and what is acceptable and unacceptable behavior for our daughters. Pornography is now so widely consumed that it is changing—in a very dangerous way—how we look at our daughters (as young women who will naturally post nude photos) and how they look at themselves. But pornography does not mirror healthy sexual behavior. It is a corrupting force—especially when it comes to our expectations of young people.

Recently, I was at a large medical conference discussing sexual activity among teens. The organizers of the conference asked five teens to sit on stage and enlighten us doctors about the stresses they face. One girl was pregnant. She said that she had been sexually active because she thought it was the only way to keep boyfriends loyal—only she learned that it didn't. Now she was soon to be a single mother. She was fearful for the future, but happy to have her baby—to have someone to love.

The second girl, a high school junior, had chosen not to be sexually active and was happy with her choice because she found that she could still have friendships with boys without having to worry about the possible physical and emotional trauma of getting pregnant.

The third girl, a high school senior, had been sexually active as a freshman, but realized it was a mistake and stopped. Some damage, however, was already done. She had been diagnosed with pre-cancer of the cervix, which required surgery and meant that any pregnancy she had in the future would be high-risk.

The fourth teen was a boy who said, "What girls don't understand is that guys don't see sex as a commitment. If a girl has sex with a guy, he thinks she's a slut, and he just wants to move on."

The first four teens had spoken while sitting down. The final teen was a seventeen-year-old boy. He shot up from his chair and marched to the edge of the stage, giving the five hundred physicians in the room an unnerving stare. He said he had never had sex, but he knew why other teens did. "Do you want to know why? Do you know what our real problem is?" He swept his index finger over the audience. "Our real problem is *you*! We have sex because you don't believe in us enough to tell us the truth!" Then he turned and sat down.

There was dead silence in the enormous room. I don't know how many of my colleagues would admit it, but he was right. As doctors, we should have been leading advocates encouraging teens to avoid sexual activity. At their stage of physical, mental, and psychological development, such activity can be heartbreakingly dangerous. And did we? No, for the most part. Most doctors, like most educators, accept teen sexual activity as a given, and our job is damage control: keep them from getting pregnant and keep them using condoms and the birth control pill. Many doctors even believe they should do this behind the parents' backs. It didn't used to be this way, but it has been this way now for two generations. The bottom line is that educators and physicians haven't believed in teens enough to respect them with the truth or expect them to be capable of self-control.

Too many parents do the same—but you shouldn't. Your daughter is fully capable of saying no to sexual activity, and if she does, her chances of a healthy physical and emotional future are immensely enhanced. Not only do we have an epidemic of sexually transmitted diseases in this country, but we also have an epidemic of depression in young people—and much of it is directly the result of premature sexual activity. Don't let that happen to your daughter.

Loneliness and Depression

Girls who engage in premature sexual activities often suffer from low self-esteem, which can degenerate into feelings of sadness, failure, worthlessness, and isolation. Her sense of isolation can be exacerbated by social media usage that replaces real, true friendships with virtual ones. Photos and texts are no substitute for real human interactions—and they can also be deceitful, leading young people into bad and unhealthy relationships. Most adults can understand this, but most kids can't. They think social media is harmless, that virtual friendships are no more hazardous than real ones, because they don't have the cognitive sophistication to go beyond their own immediate experiences and feelings—which is why most kids don't recognize the dangers until something bad happens. Depression can creep up on girls as their screen time increases, and virtual relationships—which can easily be shallow and deceitful—displace real friendships.

But remember that our daughters' screen time is only part of the problem. Another part is the screen time of *parents*. In her book *Alone Together*, Professor Sherry Turkle notes that kids want to spend more time with their parents, but feel that their parents are addicted to their phones.[4] In my own pediatric practice, I have heard the same lament: kids want attention and a close relationship with their parents, but they often feel ignored by parents who would apparently rather text friends than engage with their children (or that's how their children see it). When families are alone together—when everyone is off in a separate room texting instead of gathered around the dining table to eat, talk, or play a game—we lose sight of what it means to be truly human, and we put the emotional, mental, and even physical health of our children at risk.

What Every Parent Can Do

But let's move on to the good news. No matter how ignorant you are about social media and technology, you are far more powerful than any screen your daughter sits behind. No one and nothing—not social media, not her peers—has more influence and impact on your daughter's life than you do as a parent.

The very fact that you are reading this book shows that you care about your daughter. That means you are an attentive parent, and girls with attentive parents are far less likely to be depressed or sexually active. Part of that attentiveness needs to be used toward setting the rules about screen time.

If your daughter does much of her homework on a computer, she might have trouble concentrating on her work. She might be easily distracted by wanting to check social media. So establish a strict division between time spent doing homework on the computer and entertainment on the computer (or social media screen time). The latter could be a reward for the completion of the former. You might consider putting her computer in a public room close to you so that you can see what she's doing and encourage her to stay on task (something that many kids find challenging).

Set a limit of thirty minutes per night on non-essential screen time that everyone follows (including you). If thirty minutes is too severe of a drop, begin decreasing the time by increments of fifteen minutes until you reach the amount of time you think is appropriate. Have a cupboard or basket where everyone is required to put their phones, iPads, and laptops when they're not in use. If your daughter reacts to these rules by throwing a temper tantrum, screaming, telling you that you are a horrible, controlling parent, and insisting that no one else has these sorts of rules, don't listen. That temper tantrum itself will tell you that she spends far too much time on her screen. Screen time can become an addiction, so you need to help her better manage her time and get control of her life. She likely can't do this by herself—it's hard for teens—but with your help, she will benefit and the addiction will go away.

Unfortunately, many parents don't discuss the dangers of phones, the Internet, or social media with their kids because they assume that kids already know about them—the kids, after all, are often more tech savvy than their parents. But while they might be technologically proficient, their understanding of the broader implications of screen time is almost certainly lacking for the simple reason that they are *kids*. You, as an adult, can see the risks that they can't.

You can engage your daughter by telling her that while you understand the appeal of screen time—and have felt its pull yourself—we can never let screens take over our lives or control us. You should work with her to come up with ways to ensure this won't happen. It is ironic that while many kids spend a lot of time on social media, if you ask them how they feel about it, they feel bad. You can talk about some of these negatives—about how it not only is a waste of time and gets in the way of healthier, better, more fulfilling relationships and the enjoyment of life, but how it also can lead to truly bad things like "sexting" or emotional abuse.

One of the best ways to teach your daughter about making good decisions is to ask questions. If she gives you an answer that you think is wrong, take the questions deeper. If she thinks that sexting doesn't hurt anyone, remind her that once she posts something, she loses all control over who sees it. Does she think that sexting is a healthy way of getting attention? Does she realize that these images never go away and that others might view them differently than she does? If you ask the right questions, your daughter will eventually find the right answers, and because she comes to them herself, she will embrace them with greater conviction and they will stick.

If both of you go on a screen diet, it will help immensely. You won't risk looking like a hypocrite, you'll have more time together, and you can help her through any withdrawal pangs. Almost inevitably, she'll quickly realize how much better she feels when she's engaged in the real world and away from social media.

Teach her to use one form of media at a time. Research shows that most teens listen to music and check their phones when they do their homework (they'll even check their phones when they're watching a movie). They do this even though it distracts them and adds to their stress levels. Constant audio-visual stimulation is unhealthy for kids; it can raise anxiety and become addictive, sort of like always craving a coffee rush—even though you're already jittery from the caffeine. Kids need times of calm; they need to learn how to concentrate and focus. If you really want to help your kids, get them away from screens and put them in front of a book, or set up a board game, or go for a hike together, or run errands together, or chat, or pray together. The fun of real human interaction is your ally in defeating the beast of screen time and in shaping your daughter into the self-confident young woman you want her to become. And remember that the best way to teach is by setting a good example.

When five-year-old Tanya came in for her kindergarten physical, I chatted with her about school starting and what she did during the summer. She was animated and cordial. At one point, she gestured toward her mother, who sat in the corner checking out Facebook on her phone. "See that—that's what we call 'the family killer,'" she said, referring to her mother's phone. Kids, even more than adults, hate being ignored in favor of a phone; they're especially vulnerable to feelings of rejection and loneliness. Never let your child feel invisible. When your daughter enters the room, shut off the television, put away your phone, and close your laptop. When you do that, you communicate that your daughter is a priority—more important to you than any electronic communication. If you do that, I guarantee you that her self-esteem will soar.

And you can set this example easily with a simple rule that is binding on everyone in the family: no phones at mealtimes—ever. This is a no-brainer, but one that many parents don't, or feel they can't, enforce. The next time you go to a restaurant, look around. You'll see silent families with everyone looking at their individual phones, or the mom and dad talking while their daughter texts, or worse—a daughter looking sullen, forlorn, and lost, while her parents check their Facebook accounts. These days it's a nearly universal problem, so set the rule: don't bring your phone to the dinner table. Put it away and give priority to your family.

If you think, as most parents do, that your daughter is a good kid, keep her that way. Protect her from social media platforms that will distort her understanding of human interaction, diminish her sense of self-worth, and make her more likely to be pressured by peers. It is sad, but true, that many parents who want their daughters to stand strong against peer pressure will themselves say that they have to give their daughter a phone because everyone else has one. No, you don't. In fact, by avoiding or limiting her use of screens, you are protecting her from the risks that those other kids are facing. Give her a phone when she truly *needs* it, not necessarily when she *wants* it. Don't let peer pressure—or tantrums—make your parental decisions for you. And don't be afraid to put protections on her devices that block inappropriate content and that give you the power to supervise what your daughter does online or on her phone. This is *not* a violation of her privacy because, as you can point out to her, there is *no* privacy in the electronic world. Girls get into trouble when they enter a "private" sphere that their parents don't see, but online predators can see. Daughters need better, closer relationships with their parents—not more disengagement and alienation from them.

The truth is that girls feel *more* loved if their parents insist on watching over them. The kids who get into trouble are the ones whose parents paid them too little attention—not too much. Tell your daughter that having an electronic device is a privilege that comes with oversight and that you will have full access to her screens. Teach her to be accountable for her time online. When any of us—adults or children—live with secrets, trouble is around the corner. Teaching your daughter to be open and honest and to focus on engaging with the people around her, rather than with screens, is an important lesson that will help her find the path to a happier, more fulfilled life.

Chapter Six

Teach Her Healthy versus Toxic Feminism

It was March 1976 at Mount Holyoke College. A group of friends and I were discussing our futures, believing that we represented a new generation of liberated women. We were driven to succeed and had chosen this all-female college for one reason: we didn't want to share the college budget with men. We wanted the first pick of science equipment, the best professors focused on us, and most of all, no distractions in our work. We were determined to excel in our eventual careers.

All but one of us had been raised by full-time mothers—and we felt sorry for them. Full-time mothers had never experienced the thrill of getting into graduate school, of getting a large paycheck, or of having many opportunities to achieve "self-realization." When our mothers graduated from college, they had two career choices: to be nurses or teachers. And they had really only one life choice: to get married and have children. How sad, we thought.

We were all about breaking down barriers that kept women's choices limited. We thought the only thing standing in our way was men. They dominated the professions, they had the best jobs, they succeeded, and they did what they liked. They didn't have to stay at home, take care of children, do housework, and be grateful if they were given an allowance.

No—they earned big money, spent it how they saw fit, and came home to cooked meals. Men lived great lives—and some of them quite obviously abused their privileges. We knew or had heard about women who had been physically or emotionally abused by men, or endured an alcoholic husband, or felt like servants in their own homes, or been dumped by husbands who had extramarital affairs. We weren't going to have any of that. We were going to be in charge of our lives and have rewarding careers. Marriage and children were an option, but only one among many.

Revolution Underway

Under the tutelage of Gloria Steinem, we learned that we had been repressed by our family and society and had suffered emotionally because of it. She encouraged women of our generation to revisit our personal histories and pinpoint how and when we had been hurt. We were to enter a journey of deep self-reflection in order to start life anew and "relearn" how to live as independent, strong women. Steinem taught us that as young women, we first had to work on self-esteem. Self-esteem was defined as belief in oneself, self-reliance, self-respect, pride, and self-sufficiency. We sopped up everything that Steinem, Helen Gurley Brown, Betty Friedan, and other leading feminists wrote. We wanted to achieve a dramatic change from women's traditional roles, and our professors, for the most part, were allies. But there were times when I had smidgens of doubt.

When final exams came, we could complete them in the order we wanted. I always took my favorite exam at the end—religion. Every semester, I took a religion class taught by a quiet-spoken professor who regularly invited groups of students home for dinner with him and his family. He warmly welcomed us every time and had a cozy fire burning in his living room fireplace. When I went there, I felt like I was back at home with my own parents, and I loved it. But sometimes I felt guilty, because the professor and his religion courses (which I loved), and his wife (who cooked our delicious meals), and their warm, welcoming, and tiny Cape Cod home represented in many ways the sort of life to which we young feminists were opposed.

There was another influence that caused me to doubt. I had grown up in the Catholic Church, and Father Robert Thomas, a family friend, had inspired me to learn more about God. He spent most of his time in South America ministering to the poor, and in some peculiar way I envied him; I sometimes thought that he was on a better path than I was.

These two kind men lived with a simplicity, humility, and sense of service and self-denial that felt increasingly foreign to me. My friends and I were determined to break through barriers we thought had been imposed upon us by men; we were focused on self-fulfilling careers that would mark us out as successful female professionals. It was all about us.

By graduation, we had our professional lives planned. I would go to medical school, my roommate would attend the University of Michigan Law School, another would go to Yale to get her Ph.D., and another planned to move to France to pursue a career in art history. None of us had plans for getting married and starting a family.

In the fall of 1980, I began medical school. About a quarter of the students in my class were women. And after having immersed myself in feminism, I was surprised to find the majority of my male colleagues kind and pleasant. Many of my female colleagues were ready and eager to compete with men on every level. We were going to break new ground— but not always in ways I had imagined.

Emergence of a Second Revolution

Early in medical school, I heard male and female students openly discuss their sexual exploits. Though we were medical students, few worried about sexually transmitted infections because, honestly, we didn't know of many. HIV wasn't around. We weren't sure why cervical cancer rates were rising, though we realized it must have something to do with sexual activity because nuns never got it. Most of us didn't know the difference between syphilis (which only sailors got) and chlamydia.

Herpes Type 2 emerged as a "Yuppie" infection during the 1980s, but we didn't take it terribly seriously. Most of my colleagues were proud of the Sexual Revolution and equated it with freedom; they didn't want to hear anything against it.

I never voiced my doubts because I was a committed feminist, but I knew I was uncomfortable with people boasting about their sex lives. I doubted that promiscuity was a good thing. My mind drifted back to my religion professor and to Father Robert Thomas, their examples and their teachings, and how it did not mesh with what was going on around me.

One afternoon, a female physician led me and a group of students around the hospital. She left us for a moment to check on a patient and returned visibly upset. She decided to share her anger. "I need to tell you medical students about an issue that many of us deal with regularly. And you women students, listen carefully. Male chauvinism in medicine is alive and well. I just spoke to a friend who is married. She and her husband have three children and she became pregnant with her fourth. Her husband wanted the baby, but she didn't feel that she could handle it at this stage in her life, so she decided to have an abortion. What makes me so angry is that she is being criticized for this! How dare anyone interfere with her personal life!" She looked directly at the few women in the group and said, "Never let anyone tell you what you can and can't do with your own body. Never let them interfere with your personal decisions. They have no right!"

At the time, I thought she was correct because what she said fit in perfectly with my feminist beliefs. But I noticed it didn't sit well with many other women who thought that feminism and its defined set of beliefs were limiting what they were allowed to think—not liberating them.

In her book *The Second Stage*, Betty Friedan wrote that by the 1980s women were immersed in a second wave of feminism. We had won some important battles toward independence and women's rights, but there was much more to be done. I remember in particular Friedan's description of the housewife, bored and trapped at home:

> Suddenly after thirty years, the husband leaves this sym-
> biotic marriage for a younger woman on her way up,
> someone who is familiar with those same battles he
> fought—his equal. It turns out that the thirty-year wife-
> nurturer has only a few thousand dollars in the bank in
> her own name. Under the new divorce law, will her house-
> wifely contribution of thirty years entitle her to equal
> share of their house, cars, whatever stocks he's bought
> (wherever he has put them)? No longer the eminent writ-
> er's wife, she will not share his future royalties. Will she
> even be invited to parties?[1]

Even at the time, I thought this was a cynical and demeaning view of how most housewives lived, and I thought it was insulting to many of the women I had known growing up—most especially my mother. She had sacrificed for me and my siblings and had worked extremely hard helping my father and taking care of us—and I never heard her complain even once. Toward the end of her life my sister asked her, "What regrets do you have now that we are grown?"

Without hesitating, she said, "None. Why? Should I?"

My mother was a woman who knew who she was and what she wanted—and her vision of herself and her life was not a feminist vision like those touted by Betty Friedan or Gloria Steinem—and I did not think that my mother had made a wrong choice in her life. I still called myself a feminist, but my doubts were growing as the feminist vision increasingly seemed to be narrow-minded and shrill—not an accurate reflection of reality.

And Then a Third and Fourth Wave

It soon became apparent that feminism, as a general movement, had been entirely victorious. Women had advanced to positions at or near the top of almost every field of endeavor and utterly dominated some fields. But this undeniable and rapid success had come at some cost.

Women felt pressure to do it all and have it all. Balancing the demands of career and family was hard—even with men stepping in to do more on the domestic front. Mothers who chose to stay home full-time with their children felt less significant because those of us who worked outside the home considered ourselves "complete women" and looked down on those who weren't. Many career women, however, also felt anxious and unhappy—encapsulated in the word "stressed"—and were often extra-competitive with each other. Here's my confession: During my second year of pediatric residency, I was pregnant with our second child and working in the intensive care unit. A friend, a female colleague, was working there too. One early morning while I was driving to work, her car passed mine on the highway. "She can't get there before I do," I thought to myself. I stepped on the accelerator and passed her in the right lane. We didn't make eye contact, but we knew we were racing each other, and she passed me again—and we were now well over the speed limit. I don't remember who reached the hospital first, and I'm sure she doesn't either, but our insatiable desire to compete and win led us to take a stupid risk. Mothers are competitive with one another. We want our kid to be better on the soccer field than our friend's child. We want our teenager to get the star role in a play, get the best scholarship to the college of her choice, and make the most goals in hockey tournaments. We do so because we want our child to have the very best experiences in life. But we also want our kids to excel so that we look like better parents. And if we are more successful than our friends are, we win.

Professional women, stay-at-home mothers, single women, divorced women—we all compete. It's a passion that surges like fire from a dragon's mouth when we're parents. The problem is, it hurts our kids.

The first two waves of feminism established the fact that women wanted equality with men in all areas, but most specifically in careers. But subsequent waves heightened the competitions *between women* to see who could make the most out of these new opportunities. Women felt that they had to be excellent in the workplace, have a sparkling home, keep in shape, cook healthy meals, and ensure that their children excelled.

We put the same enormous expectations and pressures on our kids that we put on ourselves. Super moms had to have super children. And that's where we find ourselves today. We push our children to succeed—even at things for which they might have no aptitude—because we want to brag about them, and we want them to seize every opportunity for self-enrichment and success. We tell our kids that we "just want them to have fun" when we enroll them in endless sporting activities, but they and we know better. We don't care one whit about them having fun—we want them to be the best. Who hasn't heard, *or been*, the mother exclaiming, "You just wouldn't believe it—Sally is *sooo* good. Her coach is really impressed; he says she has real talent." And Sally is only five.

We all think our children are special. I would guess that about 80 percent of parents in my practice with a child under the age of two remark on how unusually advanced their child seems to be in her speech, walking, attentiveness—you name it. But who has the heart to say, "Actually, Mrs. Cleveland, your child is simply a normal eighteen-month-old"?

The truth is that most kids are normal and most parents are normal—and for most women it is very hard to excel at both a career and at motherhood. I know this may sting, but as one who writes on behalf of children, I must speak the truth. A child will have difficulty attaching to and feeling a sense of security with a mother who works sixty hours a week at a high-stress job. And it won't help matters if that child is expected to be a superstar too in order to validate the mother's choices and prove her success as a parent.

The Fallout of Feminism

Revolutions leave casualties. Although women achieved impressive gains in education and careers, it came at the price, for many, of unhappiness, loneliness, and failed—or never started—marriages. For many of us, these were unintended consequences of the feminist revolution. Here are some of the ways our culture has changed.

Decreased Women's Happiness

Since the late 1960s (when the feminist revolution started making its biggest gains), most women's happiness has fallen, with the notable exception of black women. In one of the largest studies on this subject, "The Paradox of Declining Female Happiness," authors Betsey Stevenson and Justin Wolfers report that over the past thirty-five years, "measures of subjective well-being indicate that women's happiness has declined both absolutely and relative to men," and that this decline exists regardless of marital or socioeconomic status.[2] I can provide some theories of my own to explain the data based on what I have seen among my friends, colleagues, parents, and patients.

Increased Loneliness

Professional women entered a workplace that didn't afford the sort of authentic female friendship that our mothers knew as housewives in their neighborhoods and communities with their coffee klatches, bridge clubs, book clubs, and volunteer work. In the workplace, women might be colleagues, but they are also competitors, and most women of my generation and subsequent generations have far fewer close friends than our mothers or grandmothers did. Outside of work—and, if we're lucky, family—most of us are mostly alone.

Rise in Anxiety and Depression

There seems to be a very real link between the social triumph of feminism and a culture of ever-increasing loneliness, anxiety, and depression. These trends have risen almost in tandem (with neuroses escalating rapidly in the past decade). And although we all know that correlation does not necessarily mean causation, experience leads me to believe that in this case it might. Much of women's anxiety these days comes from their failure to meet unreasonable expectations they put on themselves, in large part because of the "you-can-have-it-all" goals of feminism. The pressure to do well is never shut off—not at the office, not at home, not as a mother—never. That can be a recipe for anxiety if you're feeling overwhelmed, or feel that you're losing control of your life, or are beset by worries. When it comes to depression, the dynamics are a bit different. At the root of depression is often a deep, internal dislike—or even hatred—of oneself. Many who have suffered trauma, a sense of failure, loss, rejection, isolation, or abuse (among many other things) are set up for depression, which can stem from feelings of guilt and hopelessness. Relentless self-criticism—driven by feminist peer pressure to meet the you-can-have-it-all standards of success—can play a part in this, leading to deep unhappiness, frustration, and confusion. The stay-at-home mom might feel that she's sold herself short; the career mother might feel that she's sold her children short. Many women feel they cannot win. They feel anxiety and depression, they feel inadequate and miserable, and they feel just plain old exhausted because feminism sets outrageous expectations for women and keeps pushing them do to more in the name of "empowerment."

Emotional Detachment

When people pursue "empowerment"—autonomy, independence, and self-reliance—they can push themselves away from intimate relationships. I've seen this happen frequently with competitive couples with demanding careers—and it can be especially noticeable in their children, who can feel detached from their parents. The mothers in such cases often harden their emotional selves to justify being away from their children, and as a result, neither mother nor child feels happy.

My purpose is not to disparage mothers who work outside the home. I am one of those mothers. And while many wonderful, attentive, and loving mothers work outside the home, we pay a price too. I was lucky that my husband could be as supportive of me as he was, and his reward was an even closer bond with our children—one that made me jealous for a while. As mothers, if we choose to (or must) work outside the home, we can still be great parents to our kids. But we need to be aware that our children's need for us is just as great as if we were stay-at-home moms, and each of us has to find a healthy way to square that circle.

Conflict Regarding Autonomy

Feminism pushed for women to become autonomous from men—and one big part of that was the promotion of contraception. That marked a social revolution, but the feminist argument ran even deeper: it denied that men and women were complementary sexes that needed each other. Gloria Steinem told us, in a much-quoted line, that a woman needs a man like a fish needs a bicycle. That's a nice quip, but it's also untrue, and as far as it has been put into practice, it has been a major source of unhappiness for men, women, and children. The best place for a child is in a family with a mother and a father. And men and women also gain from marriage and stable families where husband and wife, father and mother can rely on each other in cooperation—not in competition over empowerment or conflict over autonomy—with each sacrificing something (some of their freedom or independence) for a greater good (including greater ultimate happiness).

The Rising War on Men

Feminism, unfortunately, brought a new feeling of animosity toward men. They had oppressed us, they were boorish, they were stupid (no more "father knows best"), and every trait of masculinity was criticized. It was unclear what feminists wanted men to be. My husband supported me and did it beautifully so that we could both become doctors. In fact, our relationship became stronger when we worked harder together as a team. But as feminism became more radical, *any* dependence on men was deemed wrong (even though, in biology and psychology, men and women are *meant* to be dependent on one another). Strangely, both femininity and masculinity were discounted; the former was dismissed as too kind and submissive, and male behaviors were supposedly toxic— *except in the context of being adopted by women* (so that aggression and taking command—bad in men—was good in women). In feminist theory, men really had no positive contribution to make. If they were feminized, they were pointless; and if they were not feminized, they were the enemy, the patriarchy. Recently with the #MeToo movement, men have been branded as predators, abusing their power to exploit women.

Of course, there are *some* men who are predators, but feminism seemed to utterly ignore the overwhelming number of good men who seek to help women (as my husband helped me) and support them. We need to recognize that the cultural shift against men has been extreme—and it is taking an enormous toll *on our daughters*. If they grow up believing that no man can be trusted, how will they have solid, enjoyable relationships with their father, their brothers, their male colleagues, or with any man? This is another way that feminism has created lonelier women—by telling them that half the human race, as well as the men to whom they are naturally attracted, are the enemy.

Devaluing People

If feminism devalued men, it also demolished the value of children, who then became a lifestyle choice or accessory rather than a focal point of a woman's life. With that lowering of value came something even worse—a death sentence for inconvenient children. The egocentricity of the feminist movement lured women into believing that their self-fulfillment, as they saw it, trumped everything—including an unborn child's right to life. Of course, they usually don't phrase it that way. They talk about a woman's "right" to control her own body. But look at an ultrasound and you will see an unmistakable human being, and that child is there—in almost every case—because of a free-will choice made by the woman carrying it. Feminism is no defender of the weak; it says that if an unborn life is inconvenient to a woman, she can kill it. That's what abortion does plain and simple—it ends a life.

My point here isn't to argue about abortion, but to point out the consequences of this undeniable devaluing of human life. Feminist-minded mothers may reconcile themselves to the idea that a child has no value until it is born (or even later), but our daughters, our children, are finding this idea harder to grasp. And if they do grasp it, their entire view of life is degraded because it makes the most helpless human beings disposable objects. That's not very affirming for a child.

A similar degradation is seen in the argument that promiscuity, prostitution, and participating in pornography is a woman's right. As a doctor, I can tell you that none of these activities is healthy. No good mother would ever wish these things on her daughter. If we want to raise physically and psychologically healthy young women, we need to raise them in the belief that they have inestimable value in body, mind, and spirit—and that they should not submit to the inevitable harm that comes from promiscuity.

Promiscuity is really a matter of disrespect because it implies that our sexual union with someone else is ultimately meaningless. Such disrespect has, unfortunately, become part of our culture. Many feminist women have no respect for men, an unborn baby's life is afforded little respect and can be discarded at will, and many more men treat women disrespectfully today in part because of a harsh truth: promiscuity lowers a woman's perceived value because she is easily replaced by another. We all suffer from this culture, but our daughters suffer the most.

The War on Femininity

There is a good version of feminism that we can teach our daughters. We can encourage them to be strong and hardworking, to develop their talents to their fullest measure, and to understand that femininity is a positive, wonderful thing. We should teach them that they have great capabilities for love and compassion as women. We should teach them the awesome joys and responsibilities that lie before them if they choose to become mothers.

But ironically, feminism has discounted femininity and left women confused about who they are, causing endless debates about what is and is not proper feminist behavior. My mother's generation knew exactly what a woman was—and that was that. But feminism blurred the lines between men and women, and even touted non-feminine behaviors as superior. Many of my college friends were promiscuous because they assumed men were. They disdained wearing bras because men didn't wear them. They took on more and more of what they considered to be male behaviors in the name of "feminism."

Today we have reached a point of true evil. We have created a medical condition that previously never existed: *rapid onset gender dysphoria*. Gender dysphoria is a very real but rare disorder that in the past was found mostly among boys. But now because of "gender neutral" propaganda, we have rapid onset gender dysphoria, which is found almost entirely among girls. Vulnerable young women, often going through an awkward adolescence, are making irreversible changes to their bodies through surgery and chemical intervention because they have convinced themselves that they are "different." These feelings are understandable, but when a girl experiences them in a culture that teaches her that a defined gender is bad (neither maleness nor femaleness is good) and pushes her toward becoming gender neutral, it leaves her in No Man's Land. She wants to move toward becoming male, but she feels conflicted because she isn't sure that having a prescribed gender is necessarily a good thing. We have come to the ultimate insanity of encouraging young women to become fake men.

Mistruths about Biology

Transgenderism isn't the only biological confusion that feminism has abetted. In a more mainstream way, it encouraged women to defer childbirth and focus on their careers. Feminism also asserted that if women had children later in life, they would be better parents because they would be older and more mature.

One mother in my practice began having children at thirty-five. She was a highly revered professional and didn't want to lose the status she had gained in her company. She told me after her first was born that she wanted two or three more children and was very excited about her family's future. I recommended that if she wanted more kids, she had to keep at it because her body was aging.

"That's irrelevant and discriminatory, Dr. Meeker," she said. "I'm physically in good shape and besides, my husband and I decided that this was the time in our lives that worked best for us to have a family."

"I understand," I replied. "But here's the problem: you may feel like you are twenty-five, but your uterus doesn't. It's thirty-six now."

She appeared insulted that I put forward a biological fact and was disgusted that I had mentioned a part of her body that was aging like the rest of her. How dare I challenge her plans for her family? I hear this rationale quite often. Many women want to have children when it fits their schedule, but the problem is that biology doesn't care about their plans. It marches on. Feminists who say otherwise discount the facts of life. And that's where feminism ultimately went wrong—when it morphed from a movement of expanding career opportunities into a movement at war with biology and reality. Bringing feminism back to reality is one way to make life better for our daughters.

Where to Find a Healthy Feminism

A healthy version of feminism starts in a place that will shock—if not offend—many feminists: with God. God is the original and most powerful feminist. He created women to have inestimable value. He gave women eternal souls. He chose a woman to give birth to His only begotten Son. God's feminism suffuses the Bible—from the extraordinary leader Deborah in the book of Judges to Mary Magdalene, the first person to discover Jesus's empty tomb. There is the woman in Proverbs 31, whom God described as a bread winner, caretaker of her family, and woman extraordinaire. These are just a few of the dozens of women in the Old and New Testaments who embodied physical, emotional, and mental strength that surpassed many of the men around them. And they were given these by God Himself. In His eyes, men and women are equal with everlasting souls. As the Apostle Paul says in Galatians 3:28, God sees no distinctions because we are all one in Christ Jesus. Nothing is more empowering than to know that you are created by a loving God who wants the best for you, who can guide your path on earth, and who can bring you to everlasting life. If you want examples of healthy feminism, read the Bible—that's where we and our daughters can learn both a proper self-esteem and an appropriate humility. We should teach our daughters about the leadership and love of God. He knows our talents better than we do. It is not by looking inward, focusing on our own presumed desires, or by chasing self-fulfillment that we achieve a truly rewarding life. We must seek His guidance to find our true vocation.

When our twenty-four-year-old daughter called to say that she had decided to do mission work in Indonesia, I was stricken to the core. She had gone on many medical missions with her father to South America. I could handle South America (sort of), but she said she had prayed for God to open the door to where He wanted her to go. And the door that opened was the opportunity in Indonesia.

"I feel this is where God wants me to be," she said.

"I'm not so sure about that," I replied. "God hasn't talked to Mom yet."

But of course, she went and had a wonderful year teaching in Solo, Indonesia. When she arrived home, I asked her what she had learned.

She said immediately, "God is enough."

We can't teach our daughters truths like that; they must experience them for themselves. But we can help them get there. We can tell our daughters about the character of God. We can share stories of His love and faithfulness to women as revealed in the Bible and in our personal experiences. We can teach them that their talents come from Him, and that He will give them opportunities to let those talents flourish. And when things get hard—as they did for my daughter in Indonesia, and as they do for all of us at some point or another—we can teach them that faith in God's power can help pull us through and remind us that every test we face can be met by the strength He has given us.

Teach Them to Tap into Great Character

Faith and hard work can achieve a lot, but we should never tell our daughters that they can do anything they set their heart on doing. I could work twenty-four hours a day for ten years at figure skating and never be an Olympic skater. The fact is that we are all limited in our talents.

But one area where we are not limited is in our ability to develop great character. All of us have a great capacity to cultivate within ourselves courage, patience, integrity, and humility. These virtues help girls develop a deep sense of confidence and self-worth. The way for our daughters to make the most of their existing talents is through the application of extraordinary character—through virtues like patience (with themselves and others), tenacity (the discipline to see things through), and dedication to serving others rather than thinking always of themselves.

Many years ago, I was a resident at the Children's Hospital of Wisconsin. It was an exciting time, and I was proud that my career was taking off. But early on I learned that it wasn't all about me. One patient I worked with was a young boy with leukemia. I loved talking with him and encouraging him and got to know him well. One day, he suddenly took a turn for the worse. His fever shot up, he had trouble breathing, he was turning blue, and he could barely talk to me. We gave him oxygen, put a tube down his airway to help him breath, administered a shot of antibiotics to fight what I diagnosed as a massive infection, and immediately transferred him to the intensive care unit. As we wheeled him there, I fought back tears and tried to keep my head clear. After we settled him in, I saw his mother. He was dying and she was coming into the ICU. When I saw her face, I burst into sobs. She knew immediately what was happening. The more questions she asked, the harder I cried. Finally, through her own tears she said, "Couldn't you have done something? How could you let this happen?"

I reviewed in my head what I had and hadn't done. Maybe she was right. Maybe I could have done more. I could have checked on him half an hour earlier, and maybe he would have survived. I could have added another antibiotic just in case.

I went home that night and announced to my husband that I was in the wrong profession and was giving my two weeks' notice. No amount of money, status, or self-fulfillment in living my "dream" could keep me going.

My husband listened and didn't respond right away. But when he did, he told me that my hospital was full of sick kids who needed help.

And I was there. Being a pediatrician wasn't about me—it was about them. I had been trained to serve them. That was my calling in life. And I realized he was right. I needed to dig deeper and realize that being a good doctor wasn't an end or an accomplishment in itself; it was a way that I could serve others.

The secret to your daughter tapping into great character must come from a higher calling than self-centered feminism. Self-fulfilling work won't help her keep going. Money, improved self-esteem, a desire to perform better than friends or colleagues will take her only so far. But if she leans solely on these, she will fall short of knowing the fullness of who she is. That's why you must help her to realize that even her own life isn't all about her; it's about serving others, following God's plan for her, and clinging to His support.

Help Her Find Fortitude with Humility

Jennifer, an only child, was thirteen when her mother died. She never knew her father and had no family in her hometown who could take care of her. She moved to another city (mine) and was raised by her elderly grandparents.

For the first year and a half after her mother's death, Jennifer had a very tough time. But then I saw a fire emerge in her. A sparkle appeared in her eyes, her faith seemed renewed, and she began to fight through adversity. She worked hard at school. She grew closer to her grandparents—particularly her grandfather, who took the place of the father she never knew. Instead of focusing on the misfortunes of her life, she complimented her grandparents for working so hard to help her. I saw Jennifer mature into a lovely, confident, compassionate, and outgoing young woman who excelled in college, who liked herself well enough to love other people, and who married a wonderful young man. The key to her success was her humility. She took the focus off herself and put it instead on the grandparents who were helping her, on her faith, and on realizing that her best path forward was not to turn inward, but to be open to friendships and work hard to make something of herself.

Teach Her Assertiveness without Hubris

A low point for me during the 2016 presidential campaign was when Hillary Clinton took Donald Trump's jibe that she was a "nasty woman" and made it a point of honor, as if being "nasty" was a positive trait for an assertive, feminist woman. But it's not. No one likes people (men or women) who are obnoxiously aggressive, and when feminists say that women need to get louder and get in men's faces in order to be assertive, they're simply wrong. We respect good manners in men, and they respect good manners in us. Our culture, though, seems to be going in the other direction.

My father worked at Massachusetts General Hospital during the 1960s and became close friends with the head of the pathology department there. This colleague became the editor of the most prestigious medical journal in the world—*The New England Journal of Medicine*—and was a highly regarded teacher of medical students and residents in training. The first time I met this man, he was so unassuming that I didn't believe he could be who my father said he was. He was quiet, had a kind smile, and seemed genuinely interested in others and what they had to say.

I'll never forget my father telling me, "Meg, never let your success or strengths make you feel better than anyone else." My dad's colleague was a walking embodiment of that. He did not use his expertise to put down others or to elevate himself; he used his knowledge to teach and help others. He treated everyone he met as being of equal value to himself. He asserted himself in the sense that he used his talents to the best of his ability as he advanced in his career—and that is proper self-assertion. He did not assert himself by shouting, or being overly aggressive, or being "nasty." Feminists too often deride "niceness," but there is nothing wrong with being nice. A nice woman can also be a principled woman who stands up for her beliefs—and who does so with kindness, compassion, and understanding. Asserting your talents or your opinion can be a virtue; arrogance never is—and that's something we can all teach our daughters.

Teach Her Tolerance, Not Permissiveness

"Tolerance" is a serious issue for young girls because it is a primary value in popular culture and our schools—even though, too often, we've seen "tolerance" invoked in the name of denying people the right to a different opinion because it is allegedly "intolerant." If you are categorized as part of the "intolerant" group, you can be ostracized. And if you're in the fake tolerance group, you can become a tool of fashionable opinion, unable to think for yourself.

Real tolerance is something entirely different, and it is something we find in the Bible. Tolerance in the biblical sense means to forbear—to see past differences in order to respect and love another person. What passes as tolerance today is often a demand that we must affirm social permissiveness as morally right. It is a denial that there are at least two sides to every issue. It is an attempt to shut down debate and forbid opposition. Freedom of speech and freedom of religion are fundamental rights enshrined in America's Constitution. If we are to raise our daughters to understand the real tolerance that such a right presupposes, we need to fight against a lot of what's going on in popular culture. We need to teach our daughters what we believe—*and* what our opponents believe—and why. We should teach them that disagreement is fine because it keeps everyone intellectually sharp, and that respectful debates make us think—not just react.

When I was in high school, a close girlfriend and I were on the debate team together. Our views on politics, social issues, and just about everything else were opposites. But we were good friends and helped each other craft our opposing debate arguments. Sometimes I argued the opposing side just for fun. It was fabulous training for understanding another person's point of view. Sadly, this probably wouldn't happen in many high schools or colleges today. We have become afraid to think, question, debate, or disagree because differences of opinion are regarded as moral failings. Don't let your daughter fall into that trap. Teach her to understand her own beliefs—and to respect those of other people.

Teach Her about the Grittiness and Goodness of Love

In order to love well, your daughter needs the character and fortitude to persist when things get tough. She will need assertiveness to aid loved ones in need, and she will need real—not superficial—tolerance so that she doesn't isolate those whom she loves, but with whom she disagrees. When daughters are young, many have an idealized understanding of love. They see it as a warm feeling that will launch them into a happier realm. Romance trumps love as girls move into junior high, and many girls seek to be noticed, accepted, appreciated, and admired. In high school, if not earlier, they will know that love can be difficult, even painful. They will have dealt with rejection and perhaps seen the dissolution of their own home life—or their friends' home lives—with parents divorcing.

I have talked with many girls who admit that they hated themselves during their teen years (and sometimes before). It's hard to love others if you don't see anything to love in yourself. That's where parents come in. We have learned that love isn't infatuation or simply a romantic feeling; it is an enduring commitment, and it is the commitment that brings real joy in the long run. If we show this in our own relationships, our daughters can better understand it and emulate it.

Real love can be hard. It can mean loving when we feel like love has died. It can mean being kind when we would rather be harsh. It can mean staying firm when we feel weak. It can mean staying faithful when we are tempted to lose faith. It can mean reaching out when we would rather turn inward. But in the end, love brings goodness. It brings life. It brings fulfillment. That's what we must help our daughters understand: don't be afraid to love.

One Final Lesson: Love Men

The deep wedge feminism has driven between men and women is wrong and harmful. Feminism has pushed, pounded, and belittled men, insisting that they are the villains. But of course they aren't, and our commission to love all people doesn't exclude men. It is a travesty to teach our daughters that all men are to be feared, and it is absurd to equate a flirtatious remark with physical abuse, or wolf whistles with rape. Yes, some men behave badly, even criminally. But to say the obvious—because it needs to be said—most men don't behave badly. In fact, most men strive to be good husbands and fathers.

Teach your daughter what good men do. Show her how they behave, what they say, and how they can love well and be trusted. In her heart of hearts, she will want to love a man. She will want to love her father, brother, uncle, grandfather, and husband and be loved by them. Your daughter has an innate desire to have these loving bonds. Don't let misguided feminism sever them. Mothers—if you are married, praise your husband in front of your daughter and save your complaints about him for your friends, not your kids. Fathers—respect your daughters and know that they crave your kind words and support. Keep high standards for her and be ready to fight for your daughter if she gets into trouble.

Healthy feminism can be taught to your daughter. She won't be born with self-confidence, assertiveness, and the ability to love well, but mothers and fathers can show her the way.

Chapter Seven

Eating, Body Image, and Helping Our Daughters Strike the Right Balance

Betsy was in for her fourteen-year-old physical. Her mother was with her, and I immediately felt tension in the room. Her mother was on the edge of tears, Betsy was mad, and my attempt to make cordial small talk failed.

Betsy finally blurted out, "My mom thinks I have a problem. She's been nagging me for weeks, and she's crazy. I don't need to be here. You're so smart, you probably think I have a problem too."

"You can't dismiss me that easily," I said. "What do you think your mom is worried about?"

"She keeps hounding me about what I'm eating. She's convinced I don't eat enough. But I need to eat healthily. I'm a runner. She's never been an athlete. What does she know? What do you know?"

Her mother was tearful now, but at least Betsy's hostility had redirected itself to me.

"I know what's healthy," I said. "What's changed in your eating habits?"

Betsy scowled and said, "I'm a vegetarian, okay? I need to improve my times. My coach says I'll get faster if I get thinner."

"So what do you eat?"

"Nuts and salads mostly. But I treat myself too sometimes with candy, pizza, and pasta."

"How much do you eat?"

"A lot. Mom bugs me constantly to eat more, but I eat a ton of food."

"Hop up on my table and let me take a look at you."

When I started my exam, I listened to her heart and noted that her heart rate was unusually low. But many runners who are fit have low heart rates. I walked behind her and raised her shirt to listen to her lungs. Her vertebrae were protruding, as were her ribs and hip bones. I looked at her hair and saw that it was thinning. After I finished my exam, I looked at her growth chart and noted that over the past year her weight had fallen from the sixtieth percentile to the twenty-fifth percentile. Her height remained in the seventieth percentile.

"Betsy, I'm worried about you. You're not telling me the whole story regarding your eating."

"You're just like my mom! You're against me! You don't know what it takes to get a full ride at the University of Michigan on an athletic scholarship—and that's what I'm aiming for. And I told you—I eat a ton every day. I'm out of here." She jumped from my table and tried to yank the exam room door open, but I was standing in front of it. She yelled at me, "Get out of my way! I don't need to be here."

When she realized I wouldn't budge, she sat on the exam table, but she refused to talk or make eye contact.

I turned to her mother and said, "Betsy is badly underweight and needs our help."

Betsy bolted for the door, but I blocked her again, and when she stopped screaming abuse, I said, "Betsy, you have a life-threatening illness. If you don't listen to me and your mom, I'll have no choice but to call your coach and insist you quit running until you're healthier."

I told her mother that Betsy had all the symptoms of anorexia nervosa: food phobias disguised as "healthy eating," lies about what and how much she eats, a lowered heart rate, thinning hair, distorted body image, and twisted thinking.

"You're out of your mind!" Betsy shouted.

"Maybe, but if I didn't help you now, I would be a terrible doctor. Your weight is dangerously low. So we have two options. You can either go to an inpatient treatment center for six weeks, or you can see a counselor, follow a healthy diet, and report to me every week. Which option do you want?"

Betsy sat in silence for a good five minutes. Finally, her mother said, "I think we'll go home and talk with her dad, and I'll call you tomorrow, Dr. Meeker."

They decided to go with my second option, which I supported because I was confident that we could help Betsy and do so at a much lower cost than an inpatient clinic. But make no mistake—anorexia nervosa is a serious and life-threatening illness that can be very hard to treat. Fundamentally, anorexic patients become addicted to not eating. Every anorexic girl is terrified of becoming fat, thinks food is her enemy, and will lash out at anyone who tells her she needs to eat more.

Parents often feel guilty if their daughter is anorexic, bulimic, or obese. Although we can influence our daughters' eating habits, we cannot be fully responsible for them because many other factors—ranging from simple peer pressure, to obsessive-compulsive disorder, to body dysmorphia, to trauma, to low self-esteem, or to depression—play a role in eating disorders.

Here are some startling statistics that every parent needs to know:

- 80 percent of ten-year-old girls have been on a diet.[1]
- More than half of girls and one-third of boys ages six to eight want thinner bodies.[2]
- In 1970, the average girl began dieting at fourteen; by 1990 (and since then), the average age has been around eight.[3]
- 42 percent of girls from first through third grade reported wanting to be thinner.[4]
- 51 percent of nine- and ten-year-old girls felt better about themselves while dieting.[5]

- Many studies report that most kids (even as young as five) hold the same beliefs about food restriction as their mothers.[6]

Eating disorders such as anorexia nervosa, bulimia nervosa, and binge eating disorder can be tough for parents to recognize because the physical symptoms are often disguised and girls will vehemently deny that they have a problem with eating too much or too little. Girls with anorexia, for instance, will wear baggy clothes to hide their weight loss. And if they don't eat at home, they'll say it's because they ate too much at school or at a friend's house. Girls who suddenly gain weight from binge eating will often eat small meals in front of their parents but go on a junk food binge when they're alone—and then deny any knowledge of how they could be gaining weight. Parents need to know that denials are a sign of addiction and that eating disorders are a form of mental illness.

The three most common eating disorders in girls are obesity, anorexia nervosa, and bulimia nervosa. So let's focus on these.

Obesity

Girls and parents dislike the term "obesity" because they define it as morbidly overweight. Physicians, however, define it as someone who is 20 percent or more above their ideal weight. That leaves a pretty large spectrum.

But what is startling is the dramatic rise in obesity rates in American kids. In the 1960s, the percentage of obese kids was in the low single digits, but the rates started rising in the 1970s. And by 1999–2000, about 13.9 percent of children were obese. By 2015–2016, that number had risen to 18.5 percent.[7]

There are many possible explanations for this rise: the explosion of fast food restaurants, an abundance of junk foods, psychological stressors, less playtime outside, the rise of single-parent families, and more obese parents. All these, in my experience, seem to have played a role, but the one common denominator is that obese kids respond to stress by eating.

Thirteen-year-old Darla sat in my office alone. I noticed immediately that she had gained a lot of weight since I last saw her. I didn't have to say anything. She volunteered, "I'm disgusting. I know it. Kids at school make comments. I'm flunking PE. And can you write me an excuse so I don't have to go anymore? I mean, it's terrible. My mom says I need to go on a diet."

I replied, "Well, we can talk about that. But first—how are things going? I haven't seen you in two years. What have you been up to?"

"Nothing—I mean, the same old, same old."

"Has anything changed at school, at home?"

"Well, my mom's got breast cancer. She doesn't talk about it much, but I know she's not feeling very good. She's tired all the time. She used to pick me up at school, but now I ride the bus. I hate riding the bus."

"I'm sorry about your mother. I'm sure you worry about her."

"No, not really. I mean, what can you do? People get sick, you know? That's what my sister says. She's not living at home, and it's easy for her to say. She doesn't have to see my mom sick every day."

"Yes, that's hard. How is your dad doing?"

"Well, he works all the time. I mean, when he's home, it's great. But he travels for business, and he's not home as much as he wants to be. But, you know, I didn't come here to talk about my folks. I want you to help me lose weight. It's awful."

"What have you tried so far?"

"Well, I did those protein drinks for a few days, and I hated them. Then I just stopped eating for another few days, and that didn't work either. Plus, whenever my dad's home, he makes some great food. The thing is, he loves to eat, but he stays thin. And mom's losing weight because she's sick. And then there's me. I'm fat. I don't know what to do."

"Why do you think you're gaining weight?"

"I don't know. That's the thing—I really don't eat that much. I snack on good food. Our meals are mostly healthy, though my dad loves some junk food. Mom says he shouldn't eat it, but he does. He kind of sneaks it. One day, we were eating lunch together. We were just eating peanut butter and jelly. For some reason, I asked if I could have a bite of my dad's sandwich. He looked at me funny and finally said yes. When I took a bite of his sandwich, I realized there was a crunchy chocolate bar inside! He didn't want my Mom to know he was eating chocolate!"

It soon became apparent that when her dad was home, she splurged on junk food; when her mother had a bad day, she ate more; when she was angry—even about gaining weight—she ate more; and she rarely went outside and exercised, because as she gained weight she felt less energetic. She was both stressed and bored, and her response to both was eating—and eating the wrong things.

I told Darla that we needed to develop a weight loss plan and that we needed to involve her parents. I called her father (her mother was not feeling well enough to talk) and told him that if Darla's weight gain went unchecked, it would put her at risk for diabetes, heart issues, and many other problems. Darla's father jumped into gear and helped her tremendously. He made sure that no junk food came into the house. He talked with Darla regularly about her progress, encouraged her, and tried to be home more. In addition to this, Darla got advice from a physician I recommended who is a weight loss specialist. Over five months, Darla lost thirty of the forty pounds she had gained over the last two years.

Darla was one of the lucky ones. She knew she had a problem and had to do something about it, she took her weight-loss program seriously, and her father was able to help her. Her father's participation was crucial. Girls whose parents go on the diet (and even exercise) program with them have a much higher success rate.

If you are overweight, your daughter might have a harder time controlling her appetite too. If she doesn't sleep enough (another stress factor), she's more likely to overeat. If she doesn't drink milk (which is filling and satisfying), she's more likely to become obese (in some cases because she'll drink empty, calorie-laden sodas instead). If she's inactive and spends more than two hours a day watching television, she's more likely to become obese. All these factors and many more are why involved parents working in consultation with a doctor can make a big difference in helping daughters keep their weight in a healthy range.

Anorexia Nervosa

If obesity is a problem, anorexia in a daughter is terrifying for parents because there seems to be so little they can do. Anorexia nervosa refers to the loss of appetite that has become a neurotic condition. There are two main types of anorexia nervosa: a restrictive type where a girl simply starves herself and a binge-purge type where restrictions on food can give way to a binge, only to be followed by induced vomiting (or sometimes the abuse of laxatives).

Many girls who worry about their weight go on diets, but the symptoms of anorexia are much more particular. Some of them are obvious, including visible, dramatic weight loss; attempts to disguise the weight loss with baggy clothes; and an excessive preoccupation with weight and diet. But more subtle signs include a reluctance to eat with other people present, lying about eating habits, emotional withdrawal from friends and family, mood swings, anxiety, and depression. Stomach cramps, constipation, acid reflux, poor immune function, and menstrual irregularities can accompany anorexia, as can heart problems—including heart failure. Anorexia can be fatal. Girls between the ages of fifteen and twenty-four who suffer from anorexia nervosa have ten times the risk of dying compared to their peers.

Bulimia Nervosa

Bulimia nervosa is characterized by binge eating followed by purging, fasting, or excessive exercise. Unlike anorexia nervosa, people with bulimia can fall within the normal range for their weight. But like people with anorexia, they fear gaining weight, want desperately to lose weight, and are intensely unhappy with their body size and shape.

Many of the symptoms of bulimia nervosa come from induced vomiting and include acid reflux, a chronically sore throat, dental damage, severe dehydration, and an electrolyte imbalance (which can lead to a stroke or a heart attack).

Although each of these eating disorders is different, there are genetic and psychological factors that can make your daughter more susceptible to any one of them. If you had an eating disorder, your daughter is more likely to have one. If you have a close relative with a mental disorder, or if your daughter is a Type 1 diabetic, her risk factor is higher. If your daughter is a perfectionist who sets unrealistically high goals for herself, or if she has an inflexible personality and thinks there is only one right way to do things, or if she spends inordinate amounts of time connected to media and sees celebrities as role models, then she too might be more prone to an eating disorder.

There are also cultural factors. Where once women aspired to be like their mothers, many more girls now aspire to the looks and lifestyles of celebrities in our media-saturated culture. The problem has gotten worse with mothers adopting this same adolescent attitude, taking pride in being able to wear their teenage daughters' clothes, nudging their way into their daughters' conversations, and posting pictures on social media. Unhealthy weight-watching and competition can become a mother-daughter obsession.

Still, given all the factors in play, it is often hard to predict which girls will acquire an eating disorder and which girls won't, and under what circumstances. I had known Heather since she was two years old. When she was eight, her parents divorced. She became withdrawn and her schoolwork suffered. She had no siblings to talk to, and her parents were so full of acrimony for each other that she could not talk to them about her feelings. When Heather was eleven, her mother brought her in to see me. Heather was a beautiful figure skater and needed a physical exam to show her coach that she was healthy. Her mother was worried because Heather seemed to have lost interest in skating, never saw her friends anymore, always wanted to nap after school, and seemed somber all the time. I asked Heather if she wanted to talk privately. She said yes, and her mother agreed and stepped out of the room. I asked Heather how her skating was going. She said it was okay, but quickly switched the subject to her mother's boyfriend, Craig. She hated him, saying he was nasty and mean one minute, and syrupy and nice the next. Her mother had dated him for a year and then—over Heather's vehement objections—had allowed him to move in.

"How are you dealing with it now?"

"I don't know. I just come home from school and go to my room. Usually no one's home. But sometimes Craig comes home before my mom does."

"How is that for you? Does he talk to you? Is he nice?"

"No. He isn't. He's nice in front of my mom, but not me. He calls me 'fat ass,' 'ugly,' and sometimes 'whore.' I don't even know what that means, but I think it's bad, right?"

"Yes, it's not a nice word. How do you feel when he says those things to you?"

"Horrible. Usually I cry and go to my room. But he yells at me and tells me that I hide because I can't face the truth about myself. I try to lock my door, but he gets through. One day he even broke the lock, forcing the door open. When he did that, I was really scared." There were tears in her eyes.

"Has he ever hit you?"

"No, he just scares me to death."

"So, what does your mother do? Does she defend you?"

"She doesn't believe me. When she comes home, Craig puts on this act and acts super sweet. He helps her with dinner, cleaning up, and always asks what he can do. It's sickening. Then, when I tell her I don't want to eat dinner and that I want to stay in my room, she gets mad. I hear her talking to Craig about what she's going to do with me. She thinks I am just developing an attitude."

"I'm so sorry. Can I talk to your mother about what's going on at home?"

"No! Please don't. When I get home, she'll tell Craig and he'll really get mad. He takes everything out on me. If he's upset with mom, he yells at me. If his job was bad that day, he tells me to go to my room and not come out. He tells me that he'll take my phone away. Just random weird stuff like that."

"If you can't talk to your mom, who do you talk to? How can you deal with this?"

"I've been dieting. I thought at first it might make him stop calling me a fat ass and ugly. But it didn't. So I decided that I needed to lose weight faster. This is really embarrassing to say. You won't tell my mom, will you?"

"That depends, Heather. Everything you tell me stays between us, but if you tell me about something that is life-threatening or is a serious problem, I'll need to tell your mom."

Oddly, she seemed relieved.

"Well, a couple of weeks ago, I started going into the bathroom after dinner and getting rid of my food. I felt horrible. But then I started doing it after lunch, even at school. And now I even do it when I eat a small bite of something."

I examined Heather. She was slim, but her weight fell in a normal range, and everything else in her physical exam seemed fine, except for her teeth, which were damaged by stomach acid.

I thanked Heather for trusting me. But I was fuming inside. This little fifth-grade girl was dealing with too much pain, and her mother was apparently blind to what was happening right in front of her. So I asked Heather if I could talk with her mother.

She reluctantly agreed and said she wanted to stay in the room. When her mother returned, I told her what Heather said about Craig. At first, her mother said, "Oh, she's always saying stuff like that. She's getting ready to be a teenager. You know how kids her age can act."

"Yes, I do, and I believe Heather is telling the truth. She's not just moody, she's in trouble—physical and emotional trouble." I told her exactly why and discussed Heather's eating disorder.

"Well, I appreciate your concern, but I think you're exaggerating. Craig is a wonderful man, and any eating issues Heather has have nothing to do with him or me. Her friends are dieting, and she is too impressionable. We need to deal with that."

Heather's mother was a friend, but I had to confront her with the truth. "Heather's sick. She's suffering from anxiety, depression, and an eating disorder that if left untreated could become life-threatening. If you aren't going to get her help, I'll have no option but to call Child Protective Services."

Her mother began to sob, confessing that she knew Craig treated Heather badly and that she had made a terrible mistake in bringing him into the house. She had been lonely, she said, and wanted to make her ex-husband jealous, and now she loved Craig.

"It doesn't matter," I replied. "For the sake of your daughter, he's got to go. Today."

To her credit, Heather's mother ordered Craig to move out, and we got Heather the aggressive medical help she needed. I'm happy to say that Heather recovered and is a healthy college graduate living on her own now.

What Can We Do to Help Our Daughters?

Heather's case is instructive because to most outward appearances she looked fine physically, as many people with eating disorders do—at least initially. The good news is that if caught early enough, a complete recovery can be achieved from an eating disorder. But that also raises the question of what we can do to prevent these illnesses from arising in the first place. It begins with paying more attention to what our daughters see and hear.

Limit Their Access to Social Media

Permit me to let you in on a secret: most girls don't like being on social media as much as we think they do. Studies indicate that girls who spend more time on smartphones and social media are at a dramatically higher risk of depression, and even suicide.[8] Girls on smart-phones and social media are bombarded with unhealthy messages about their bodies—everything from pictures of Instagram models to pornography and sexting. Your daughters are on these devices because their friends are, because they think everybody is, and because screens can be addictive. But they would like nothing more than an excuse to get off these devices because they make them feel bad. We need to give them that excuse. Most parents are afraid to confront their children about curbing their social media usage, but believe me—your daughters would rather you did (even if at first they say otherwise).

The happiest kids I have seen over more than thirty years as a pediatrician are those who feel close to their parents. These are the kids who know their parents love them and are unafraid to show their love by setting rules and boundaries for them. Your relationship with your daughter—and her well-being—are put at much greater risk if you don't impose limits on her use of screens. Screens can divide kids from their parents—and that equals unhappiness.

Change the Way You Talk

While parents don't directly cause eating disorders, what we say and the example that we set can have a big impact. When a girl hears her mother continually saying things like "Oh, I'm so fat" or "I've just got to lose ten or fifteen pounds," she learns that weight is very important to her mother. Don't get me wrong—it is important that you model a healthy weight and a healthy lifestyle. But what you don't want to do is to imply that an individual's *value* is based on her appearance.

Fathers also need to be careful. It's fine to occasionally compliment your daughter on how she looks, but try to spread that out with compliments about her character. Compliment her on her patience, kindness, courage, faithfulness, perseverance, consideration for others, empathy—the list of good character qualities is long. If you merely fixate on her looks and beauty, it can backfire.

Rules about Food

The rules we should use regarding food will be slightly different depending on which eating disorder your daughter could be most susceptible to developing.

Obesity. If your family has a propensity to be overweight, here are some simple rules that can help prevent or reverse obesity:

- *Implement the "one" rule:* having one serving of food at each meal, one snack between meals, and no seconds on any foods.
- *Have everyone in the family follow the same rules.* That can be tough, but it also makes the rules easier to implement and follow. It will also prevent one parent or sibling from undermining your daughter's efforts by, for example, cooking high fat desserts or buying junk food.
- *Offer plenty of variety in foods.* If you restrict a daughter's diet to vegetables and low-fat foods and forbid carbohydrates or pasta (or other food groups), your daughter will crave what she can't have. When a girl knows that many foods are acceptable, she will feel less deprived.
- *Pack her lunch.* School meals are notoriously high in fat, salt, and calories; a healthy packed lunch might be only half the calories of a school lunch.
- *Focus on eating real foods (fish, meat, eggs, vegetables) rather than processed "diet" foods.* Real foods are more satisfying and filling, and people often eat *more* calories from diet foods because they think they can. Diet colas that contain aspartame and other additives aren't good for kids. Some may trigger health problems (like migraines) and create a craving for high-sugar products.
- *Focus on your daughter "growing into her weight" rather than losing weight.* This of course depends on two factors: the girl's age and the degree of her obesity. If she is in the

first grade and in the seventy-fifth percentile for weight and the tenth percentile for height, then she should be encouraged to "grow into her weight," which means that rather than trying to lose weight, she should focus on not gaining weight over the next few years as she grows taller. If, on the other hand, she is sixteen with her height in the thirtieth percentile and her weight is over the one-hundredth percentile, then she needs to lose weight. Most girls are fully grown at sixteen (growth stops two years after the onset of menses), so if she is overweight at sixteen, she needs to make dietary changes.

- *Don't nag.* Girls who are overweight know it. You don't need to remind your daughter because this will make her feel ashamed and like a failure. Once you and she have discussed an eating plan, implement the rules at home and let it go.
- *Exercise together.* Don't make your daughter go to the gym by herself. Go with her and do your own routine, or just take a walk or a jog together. You don't have to make it hard, but exercising together will help keep her motivated.

Anorexia or bulimia nervosa. If you suspect that your daughter is restricting foods or food groups, watch her closely. If the list of foods that she won't eat lengthens, intervene and change your family's eating habits, beginning with insisting on family dinners together. Offer well-rounded meals that include lean meats and legumes because most girls who have started diets will accept these foods.

- *Begin offering higher-fat foods.* Too much fat is bad, of course, but full-fat foods have their place in a healthy diet because they are filling and can complement nutrient-rich foods (for instance, putting real butter on vegetables). If your daughter is being overly restrictive in her diet, often one of the first casualties is necessary dietary fat. Full-fat yogurt, nuts, and seeds are foods she might accept as healthy that will provide her with the fats she needs.

- *Watch her weight—and how she eats.* If you see that your daughter is changing clothing sizes, losing energy, and moving food around her dinner plate without actually eating it, she may need to see a doctor.

- *Don't be the food police.* Stress is a common cause of eating disorders, so you want to make eating as stress-free as possible. Set the rules—and if you need help, get it from a physician and let her doctor keep her accountable for her weight and food intake.

- *Watch for vomiting.* Girls with a binging and purging type of eating disorder will try hard to hide it because they are ashamed of their behavior. They will often excuse themselves immediately after dinner and go to the restroom. While everyone else is still talking round the table, they will be vomiting.

- *Pay attention to her exercise.* Many girls with anorexia and bulimia become obsessed with exercise. Your daughter might start slowly, working out three times a week for thirty minutes. Then she will increase the frequency to every day—and exercise for longer and longer periods of time and lie about it. Remember that lying is part of the disease. If you exercise with your daughter, you can prevent excesses. But if her exercise gets out of control and is something she hides from you, then you will need outside help.

Again, many of the factors that drive eating disorders are beyond your control. But what you can control, you should. And there is no reason why you should not give your daughter the best protection you can—which is your unstinting love, parental guidance, and good example.

Chapter Eight

Root Her Faith in God

Since I'm a pediatrician, let me start this chapter with some startling data on the impact faith has on our health. One massive survey of scientific literature[1] discovered that:

- 93 percent of scientific studies showed that faith gave people more meaning and purpose in their lives.
- 68 percent showed that people with faith have higher self-esteem.
- 44 percent concluded that people with faith have a greater sense of self-control.
- 56 percent of studies indicated that people with faith were less likely to be depressed and were quicker to recover from depression.
- 80 percent of the studies showed that people with faith were less likely to attempt suicide.
- 78 percent of the studies found that faith reduced anxiety.
- 86 percent showed that people with faith were less likely to engage in risky sexual behavior.

- 69 percent correlated faith with a lower chance of heart disease.
- 62 percent found that people with faith had lower, healthier blood pressure.
- 57 percent of the highest quality studies found that people with faith had better cognitive functioning.
- 71 percent of the studies discovered that people with faith had better immune function.
- 55 percent said that faith correlated with a lower risk of developing cancer and a better prognosis for recovery.
- 75 percent found that faith was predictive of a longer life span.

I can show you one excellent study after another about why religion is good for your daughter's health. It helps her live longer, reduces her risk of smoking and engaging in other unhealthy activities, and has so many beneficial qualities that it could count as a wonder drug. In addition to keeping your daughter healthy, it can make her happier, give her a deeper sense of purpose in life, and add immensely to her sense of personal value. These are no small things. They are, in fact, central to your daughter's future. Faith works because it grounds your daughter. Agnostics and atheists dismiss faith as wishful thinking or a fairy tale. But from what I've seen, faith will give your daughter a healthy sense of realism—an understanding that she is a part of a larger whole and that everything is not all about her.

When she's not grounded in that sort of realism, when she thinks life is indeed all about her, she's set herself up for trouble. I've seen it a thousand times—women who grew up seeking self-fulfillment and got everything they wanted, only to end up a victim of depression and anxiety. The pursuit of self-fulfillment is not a healthy lifestyle in the end. It doesn't bring happiness. From what I've seen, it most often brings misery. The happiest people are the people who have a sense of purpose in life—and that purpose must extend beyond themselves.[2]

Most parents know deep down that this is true. We know that money, fame, good looks, and professional success aren't enough to make a person happy—and yet more often than not, we push out daughters to pursue all these things: social popularity, high achievement, the six-figure salary. These things aren't bad in and of themselves, but they should never be our primary goal or motivation because failure to achieve them can be soul-crushing. Ironically, achieving these goals can be just as problematic because once they are obtained—what then?

Our daughters might be smart and kind, and they might be great businesswomen and wonderful mothers, but unless they understand their purpose in life and see it as something bigger than themselves, they will not ultimately be happy. Life will seem somehow empty; their victories will seem somehow hollow and transient because our daughters need to know they are part of something more—something of lasting value and meaning.

And that begins with teaching them that their lives are not all about them; they are about serving God. He is the One who made us. He is the One with a plan for us. He is the One fitting us into the whole. The Apostle Paul said that God is before all things, and in Him all things hold together (Colossians 1:17). In this context, we can better understand Saint Augustine's famous opening to his *Confessions* where he praises God and observes, "You have made us for yourself, and our heart is restless until it rests in you."[3] Your daughter will always be restless, will always be unsatisfied, will always be unfulfilled until she finds faith. And the road to faith is a search for truth.

A Desire to Seek the Truth

Young children come to faith naturally. They know they are limited, and they know there are powers greater than themselves—beginning with their parents, and leading ultimately to God. Children also possess an uncanny ability to uncover what is true and right and good. They have an instinctive sense of morality. They know that children should not hit each other (if they see another child do this, they know it is wrong). They know that adults shouldn't scream at each other (and they lose respect for those who do). But as they get older, truths and certainties get muddled. Sometimes doubts begin with a trauma, such as parents divorcing, or verbal or physical abuse from their parents. Sometimes doubts begin because of peer pressure—when friends tell them that their parents' values are all wrong. Sometimes religious doubts come from the hypocrisy of religious people who can be judgmental and cruel and fail to practice what they preach. I have repeatedly heard folks say, "I'm not interested in Christianity because it has hurt so many people." I get it.

But the solution comes from professors Peter Kreeft and Ronald K. Tacelli. They write, "One of the few things in life that cannot possibly do harm, in the end, is the honest pursuit of truth."[4]

Over the past fifteen years, I have personally witnessed a change in young people's attitudes toward life, morality, and God. Many critics say that millennials are self-centered, not interested in working hard, and definitely not interested in religion. That's not what I have seen. They might appear more self-centered and less hard-working because it can be hard for those of us from a different generation to distinguish between their electronic entertainment, electronic work, and electronic engagement with intellectual ideas (such as listening to podcasts). But I have found through talking with young people that many of them are engaged in a search for truth. Some have abandoned religion because they see it as superficial—in large part because they have seen it practiced by hypocrites—and young people can be unforgiving of hypocrisy. But a deeper quest for truth can lead to a better-rooted faith.

I have a patient in my practice, Eliana, whom I adore. I know it's not right to say things like that about a patient, but I have been with her for the past nine years and have seen her go through tremendous struggles. And in those struggles, she has been completely alone. Her parents are divorced. Her father lives far away and has a new family, including three young children. Her mother was rarely home, spending her time working or staying with a boyfriend. Her brother left home when he was sixteen. Her older sister has a severe mental illness and is institutionalized. From the age of thirteen onward, Eliana spent a lot of time home alone.

She has gone through depression, incapacitating anxiety, and even been suicidal. When she was fifteen, she shaved her head and had her forearms tattooed. I hardly recognized her. She told me that she did it to get attention—both from a new set of friends and from her mother. Her mother called her "just another rotten kid."

Eliana sobbed at the memory and said, "Here's the thing, Dr. Meeker—life is just miserable. I'm so anxious I can barely function at school. My friends make fun of me, and my mom could care less whether I live or die. I mean if there is a God, I'm sure He wouldn't like me either."

Eliana barely graduated from high school. Then she got a job waitressing. I didn't see her for three years. Technically by then she was too old to be seen by a pediatrician, but at twenty-one, she visited me as a patient one last time.

When I opened the exam room door, her appearance had changed dramatically for the better. Her hair had grown out and her face was full of excitement and life.

I said, "Eliana, you look great. You look happy. What's changed?"

"Well, Dr. Meeker, here's the thing: When I was fourteen, you asked me if I believed in God, and I said no and got all upset. But something happened when I turned nineteen. I looked back over my life and realized that if I was going to get beyond the misery, I had to figure some things out. It started when I met a new friend, a girl at work.

"We had a lot of fun together and became close and talked about how we had both struggled in life. We tried to help each other, setting each other up on dates and stuff. One day my friend said, 'I've been with so many people and tried so many things. I just don't know what's true and what isn't, what's right and what's wrong, if there's really more to love than hooking up.' And I couldn't answer her. But I wanted to.

"I started thinking about my own life—how I'd once almost killed myself and how something I can't explain stopped me. I decided to figure some deep things out. Why was I here? Why had I gone through everything I had? Was God real, was love real, and was there more to life than I knew? I began reading and asking questions. I went to a few churches and heard them talk about how important it is to obey God and pray, but those sermons didn't do anything for me. I had to find the answers on my own."

"So where did you go to find them?"

"I read—a lot. Since I never believed in God, I started with the atheists, like Richard Dawkins. I wanted to know why they didn't believe either. Then I read stuff by C. S. Lewis, Henri Nouwen, and even the Bible sometimes. At one point, I even started praying. Can you believe it? But I felt desperate. Something had to make sense. There had to be a point about life. And I was determined to find it."

"Did you?"

"Yeah, I did. I mean, I didn't understand everything, but I eventually decided that the one thing I did believe is true is that God is real. He really is. He makes sense. A lot of Christians don't, but He does. So I prayed and asked Him to show me He was real. And He did. I had a series of dreams that all fit together. And in one, I saw Jesus walking down a street with a woman running after him. She was yelling and he didn't hear her. Finally, she ran fast and got in front of him. She was mad and said, 'If you are God, then what's the matter with you? Why haven't you been there for people? Why have you been absent, silent?' Then He said to the woman, 'If I had shown myself to you, would you have come after Me?' That's when I knew that He was real. He was there all the time. He was the One who helped me survive, who kept me from committing suicide, and who was waiting for me to find Him—and now I have."

She saw God as her spiritual Father. She looked to Him for guidance. She had found in Him her sense of meaning and purpose, and she finally felt fulfilled and happy. And as the years have passed, her faith has remained strong, providing her with direction.

Finding a Healthy Perspective

I understand that many parents are uncomfortable with the idea of faith, and I understand that many people reject the idea that one religion or another has a certain claim on truth. But I write these words as a convinced Christian. I am convinced because of two things: First, years of study have convinced me that the Old and New Testaments represent real history and tell a cohesive, prophetic story that makes sense. Second, Christianity offers the best explanation I have found for explaining what it means to be human.

Many young people today are unfamiliar with the Bible, biblical history, theology, and philosophy. They are focused on professional success and the academic subjects they think will get them there. Yet when they are given the opportunity to discuss these things, they jump on it. When a Christian apologist like Ravi Zacharias, or Abdu Murray, or Os Guinness is asked to speak at the University of Michigan or Harvard or Berkeley or Yale, the auditoriums are packed. That's because we all want answers to life's deepest questions—and young people want that more than most because they haven't come to their own conclusions. Many are troubled by the culture they see around them on campus of promiscuity, pornography, and boys addicted to drinking and computer games. It seems shallow because it is. Many work hard to succeed academically so that they can get a good job and pay off their college loans, but they yearn to have answers to the bigger questions that go beyond getting good grades and earning a living. Do they have a purpose beyond themselves? Some of course will flatly say no—or live as if they believe that while focusing on dieting, exercising, clothes, grades, hooking up, and developing their professional talents. But the inquisitive ones might not be satisfied with an answer that reduces everything to self-interest.

That's where God comes in. He provides a new perspective—one that looks beyond the self and that ties an individual's life to eternity; one that says we were born to love and to be loved and that all of us, from the lowliest to the highest, have infinite, unconditional value; and one that says we should serve each other and live by a moral code that respects our neighbor, ourselves, and the God who created us. God affirms your daughter's sense of conscience. He gives her strength and confidence when she needs it most.

Almost every parent I have met in the past ten years has expressed worry over the world in which our kids live and the terrible influences around them. Yet few know how to help their daughters. They can't help as long as they accept popular culture and see life through its perspective; if they do so, they simply can't teach their daughters why hooking up is bad, why watching porn hurts her, and why feeling so anxious about her life is unnecessary.

The only way we can help our daughters is to teach them to see their lives through God's perspective, which is one of perfect love. That love means there is no need to fear, that love can be a shield against those who would degrade her sexuality and her humanity, and that love can inspire a true commitment to family and to God Himself.

Experiencing Peace

The Apostle Paul counseled, "Be anxious for nothing, but by prayer and petition, make your requests known to God" (Philippians 4:6). This passage is something that every girl struggling with anxiety needs to hear.

Next to love, peace is what most people want—but they don't know where to find it. Anxiety is a chief factor behind abusing alcohol, taking drugs, and suffering from eating disorders. Those who seek peace in the wrong places often do so because they doubt God is real or that He cares about them. Finding God's peace requires trust and faith, as well as a willingness to seek Him out through prayer.

The greatest demonstration of peace I ever experienced came from Renée's family. The day I started my pediatric internship, I was assigned to Renée. She was eight years old. She had fallen into a swimming pool and been drowning for five to ten minutes before someone saw her and pulled her out.

After several days in the intensive care unit, she was transferred to the floor where I was working. When I first saw Renée, she was lying flat on her back and her eyes were closed. She was in a coma. A young woman sitting next to her and holding her hand said, "She's been like that ever since the accident."

I introduced myself and said, "I will be taking care of Renée for the next two months. Are you her mother?"

"Oh, no—I'm her Aunt Louise. I just come and sit with her to give her folks a break."

Later that evening, I met Renée's parents, and I was struck by how calm they were.

Week after week, her father, mother, aunt, and other family members and friends kept vigil over Renée. I remember finally lamenting to a colleague, "They really think that Renée's going to get better. Someone needs to tell them that she's not. Who knows what state her brain is in? She hasn't had a brain scan is a month."

A few days later, I went into Renée's room and told her parents, "We need to talk about Renée. I'm worried that she may not get any better. We know that statistically a patient with her level of injury after this length of time may never improve."

My words didn't rattle their calm; Renée's mother even seemed to smile as if in thanks for all we were doing. I confess that I thought they were delusional and couldn't handle the truth.

I checked on Renée every day to make sure that she was nourished and that her vital signs were stable. Every time I went into her room, there were three or four people sitting by her bed.

I tried talking to her parents again to prepare them for the worst, but to no avail; they refused to believe it. I spoke to my senior resident about Renée and said, "You know and I know that she's not going to get any better, but her parents and her relatives just won't accept that."

"I know. I've been watching them. It's odd that they don't seem to understand. But her mom and all those visitors are praying for Renée."

I moved to a surgical floor for two months and then the oncology unit for another two. I was having lunch with a friend who was working on Renée's floor. I asked the question that I didn't want her to answer I asked if Renée had died yet.

"Died? No! She's up and eating in her bed."

"There's no way that she could be awake—let alone eating."

"Well, she is. Go see for yourself."

And I did. Renée was sitting up in bed and her parents were holding her hands. She couldn't talk, but she could nod and smile.

"Hello," I said, "I don't know if you remember me."

"Dr. Meeker, of course we remember you. How are you doing in your new assignment?"

"I'm sorry about what I told you a while back—about her not getting any better. This is just so unusual," I said.

Renée's mother replied, "Dr. Meeker, we are people of faith. We know we can't make our daughter better. But we know God can. So we just pray. In prayer we find comfort, closeness to God, and hope. Do you know what I mean?"

"Did you think God would heal Renée if you prayed hard enough?" Her answer surprised me.

"Not necessarily. He has His plan; it may not be ours, but because He is good, whatever happens will be okay."

Several months passed. One day, I was on Renée's floor and decided to see her, but she wasn't there. I went to the nurse's station and asked whether Renée had been transferred to another hospital. "Oh no, Dr. Meeker—she went home."

"She went home?"

"Yup—as soon as she was walking and talking and eating well on her own, her doctor discharged her."

I felt like a witness to a miracle. I've seen many parents pray for a loved one to be healed and have prayed for many myself. Sometimes they got better and many times they didn't. I don't know God's will or how prayers work with Him.

But here's what I do know for sure: I saw God give Renée's parents extraordinary peace. They weren't just mild-mannered; they had serenity. They were calm and trusting because they had faith in a good and loving God. And I believe Renée's recovery was a miracle.

Several months later, I bumped into Renée's mother. She told me that Renée's recovery was continuing. But she wanted to tell me something more. She said knowing God and having faith was one thing, but following Him was another. And then she said something I will never forget. "Dr. Meeker, in your profession, you will see many children. When you look at them, you will see the image of God stamped all over them."

And I have. In fact, in thirty years of pediatric practice I have never met a child I didn't like. I've worked with some really difficult teens. But the more obnoxious they act, the more clearly I saw the small child curled up inside asking for help.

Renée's mother encouraged me to become more serious about my faith, which I took to heart. I began to attend church regularly, which was something I had fallen away from because I was "too busy." I learned to seek God's will for my life every day, to surrender to that will, and to do what it asked. And I found that it worked.

The peace Renée's mother had was real and based on a deep faith—not something that you could just talk yourself into believing. I came to see that peace was something that God *gave* her. It doesn't come easily or by accident. We must seek it from God. That means that we need to ask for it. I know what grief looks like, and I know that peace and hope come from a transcendent, merciful God.

What's a Parent to Do?

You might think, "Faith is great for some parents, but you don't know what I'm up against." Or perhaps you're a skeptic and think, "Come on, this can't be real. I don't believe in God, the Bible, or prayer. What is a parent like me supposed to do?"

To which I would say, "Trust me. We don't know one another, but I have met you among the thousands of parents I have met over the past thirty years. You are one of them: the evangelical, angry because your prayers have not been answered in the way you expected; the atheist, dismissing talk of prayer as irrelevant; the agnostic who is simply exhausted and can barely get her children to bed on time—let alone teach them about God; the deist who believes there is a God, but thinks that

He is essentially unknowable and uninterested in us. And I have met your children—the infants and the teens, the well-behaved kids and the runaways. I know your challenges—and I've seen what works for kids."

Here's the good news: whatever we may believe, we all want certain things for our daughters as good, devoted parents.

First, *we want our daughters to be happy in life*. Money, fame, and success have their benefits, but they aren't the source of happiness. Keep that in mind when you're raising your daughter. There is no need to push her into endless competitions—academic, athletic, or otherwise. One of the biggest mistakes parents make is to assume that their children will hate them if they don't push them to excel. Actually, the reverse is true. Kids with demanding parents are often the ones who get burned out and feel resentful. All your children need from you is your love and patient guidance. For many, the model for that comes from God—the true source of all real happiness.

Second, *we want our daughters to stay away from trouble*. We don't want our daughters pregnant at sixteen, hanging out with the wrong crowd, smoking cigarettes, taking drugs, or flunking out of school. And the fact is that God makes kids better. The data show this, and so does my experience as a pediatrician (and as a mother of four): kids with a firm faith in God are far less likely to harm themselves or others. God is good for kids.

Third, *we want our daughters to be successful*. The trick here is to define success and to be honest with yourself. Are you assisting your daughter toward a goal that she wants? Or are you pushing her toward a goal that you want and that will make you feel like a successful parent? Even more important: Are you making her happiness and identity dependent on her success? That's where many parents get into trouble. Success is not a vehicle that your daughter can ride to find happiness. It often won't get her there. Success and happiness start with your daughter being the best person she can be—a person with strong character and compassion. Faith in a loving God can help her be that person. It can help her find her purpose and her vocation in life, whether it's to be the CEO of

a large company, a nurse, or a stay-at-home mom. True success and happiness come when we do what we believe we were born to do.

Fourth, *we want our daughters to have good morals*. If she doesn't
know God, this is going to be a tough one. You can teach her either that
she can find her own moral compass (which can mean adopting that of
her peers) or that she should follow yours. We all know that a child's
most common question is "why?" So if your morality isn't rooted in some
greater authority, she might just make up her own. Or you can go to God.
I have watched thousands of girls grow up. I have seen great kids come
from bad parents and bad kids come from good parents. I have seen
privileged girls in the depths of depression, and girls from difficult backgrounds who turned out well. I can honestly say that it is the girls with
religious faith who are the ones most likely to have good relationships
with their parents, confidence in themselves, and hope for the future.

Five Ways to Teach Your Daughter Faith

In his beautiful work *Pensées*, Blaise Pascal wrote that there are three
kinds of people in the world: those who serve God, having found Him;
those who are occupied seeking Him, not having found Him; and the
remainder who live without seeking or finding Him. The last category
is one of ignorance or rejection. The second category, given human weakness, could be an endless search. The first category is the one that will
root your daughter and give her strength for her life ahead.

One: Take Inventory of Your Own Faith

God can do remarkable things in kids' lives. I've seen it—and so have
they. I have had many kids tell me that they have seen angels—and no,
they weren't on morphine at the time. And I know that for many girls,
God is someone who is kinder, gentler, and smarter than anyone else,
and they believe they can talk to Him through prayer when they don't
want to talk to anyone else. God gives our daughters something real to
hold on to—something that, with faith, they will never lose.

It's a lot easier to teach your daughter about God if you know who He is. In my experience, those who genuinely seek God find Him. That's certainly the way it is for children. Their faith is instinctive, and when they seek God, they do so genuinely. They don't have our hesitation, suspicion, or doubt. So take inventory of your faith. Your daughter might even be ahead of you. But over time, her first principles will likely be your own.

If you already have a strong faith, I'm going to challenge you: Do you live your faith in a way your daughter can see? Having a strong faith is a tremendous gift. But unless we live our faith out fully, it can make our daughters bitter and cynical if they see that we cut corners and are hypocrites. How your daughter sees God may largely depend on how she sees you (especially if you are her father). So you'd better stay on your toes.

Two: Model Your Faith

Remember that it's not about putting up a good front for your daughter. If you are skeptical about faith, tell her. Don't fake it, because it won't work. Daughters have an uncanny way of reading their parents. They know within three minutes of you walking into a room what kind of mood you are in. If you do have faith and want to set a good example for your daughter, the best thing you can do is read, study, pray, and ask God to help you.

Parents often lament that their kids are nice to other people, but not to them. Kids will tell me almost the same thing—that their parents are nice with other adults, but get frustrated and angry with them. Life is stressful, and we all have our weaknesses. But if we recognize those weaknesses, we can change them. If you recognize that you are an irritable, short-tempered, and angry parent, ask God to help you become kinder and more patient. I have had parents tell me that they have done this—that they sincerely and repeatedly got down on their knees and prayed about it—and that their prayers have been answered.

Abby told me about a change she saw in her mother. In the past, her mother had been rarely home. And when she was home, she and Abby fought so much that by the time Abby was fourteen, she told me that she wanted to live with her grandmother or aunt instead of with her mother. They argued over schoolwork, friends, how often she used her cell phone, and what time she went to bed. As far as Abby was concerned, there were no nice times they had together. Abby thought that her mother was a Christian hypocrite. "She spends more time at Bible study than she does with me. In her eyes, I don't count. And I'll bet that when she meets with her friends, she acts as nice as she can be."

One day after church, Abby's mother decided she was going to join a friend for a week-long mission trip to help at an orphanage in Guatemala. Her mother asked Abby if she wanted to go too. Abby replied, "No way, Mom. It would be torture to be away for a week with you and your friends."

Weeks passed before the mission trip, and Abby saw pictures of the children at the orphanage. She felt sorry for them, and after a few days, Abby asked if she could go on the trip too. And she did.

Several weeks after they came home, I saw Abby. She seemed more confident, happier, and made eye contact more easily than she had in the past.

I asked, "How was Guatemala?"

"It was really great. The children were terribly poor, but they were so happy to see us. We just held them, kept them company, and played games with them."

"How was it being with your mom for a week?"

"Well, at first I was mad. I thought that this was all about looking good to her friends. But I saw a new side of her there. She seemed devoted. She was always calm. She smiled a lot, and always asked me about my day. I had never spent so much time with my mom, and we talked more than we ever did."

"What did you learn there?"

"About what?"

"About yourself, about your mother."

"Well, I learned I can do more than I thought I could—and this will sound weird, but I felt nicer, like I'd become a better person."

"And what about your mom? Did you get along okay?"

"You know, Dr. Meeker, that was the most amazing part about it. We did. The more time we spent together, the more we got along. It was tough down there. The food was terrible. We slept on the floor of a gym. We had to travel hours on a dirty bus. But we had a great time. And I saw her faith was real—it had to be to do things like that. You know what I mean?"

"So let me ask another question. Did being there change your faith?"

"Yeah, it did. I know this sounds weird, but I think I really saw God. I mean, not like in the sky or standing next to me, but something made me feel that He is real and He cares for all of us—even for me."

Kids *hear* our words, but it is when they see us *live* those words that they are changed. That's what Abby saw in her mother on that trip—and it was a transformative experience for her.

Three: Help Her Seek God

Young children seek God, and we should encourage that search by reading appropriate Bible stories in children's editions to them and being ready to answer their questions. The Bible, of course, is a serious book, and some of it requires maturity to fully understand. But there are other stories, like *The Chronicles of Narnia*, that can be effective in teaching children about faith and its virtues with symbolism that they can understand easily.

As your children get older, you can read the Gospels together. I particularly recommend the Gospel of John. And you can read books of apologetics like *The Case for Christ* by Lee Strobel, *More Than a Carpenter* by Josh McDowell, and *Jesus on Trial* by David Limbaugh, as well as Christian self-help books like Rick Warren's *The Purpose Driven Life*. The best faith is a well-informed faith.

Four: Pray with Her

Many parents are squeamish about praying with their daughters. In fact, most daughters, particularly if they are young, love having their parents pray with them. I have two-year-old twin granddaughters who, if we forget to pray before a meal, remind us.

Prayer has a way of bringing families together. One obvious way is if you hold hands before saying grace. Even if you've had a tough day, that moment of human contact and unity in prayer can make a big difference. Praying with your children is one of the best ways to get close to them.

When you pray with your young daughter, teach her that God is always available to her through prayer. He is kind and good and cares about her and can help her. And if she's older and won't pray with you, pray for her alone, but *tell* her that you are praying for her. *Ask* her if she has a prayer request. Don't be surprised if, over time, that request is to pray with you.

I have wanted many of my patients to know that they can grab onto God when they need support. Many troubled teens feel that no one sees them—that no one cares about them, listens to them, or loves them. I have asked many of them, "Tell me, who in your life loves you?" And sadly, many kids look at me with a blank stare. "Well, maybe my mom, but I'm not sure. Aside from her, there's no one."

Love is the foundation for a good life, and if love isn't part of a girl's life, then she feels she has no life. Sometimes troubled girls have difficulty understanding that God loves them because their experience is that no one loves them. Troubled girls in particular need to know that they can always turn to God. He is always there. He always loves them. They can always talk to Him in prayer.

Prayer gives your daughter time to open up. It's hard to pray and hide things from God. Since God knows what's going on anyway, many girls feel the freedom to pray about things that they would never talk about with their friends or with you. Girls need to verbalize how they feel—an inability to do this is often a symptom of depression—and prayer affords them the opportunity to talk through their feelings. Prayer is a way for all girls—troubled or not—to bring their worries to God. And they can bring Him their happiness too, which encourages gratitude and appreciation. Prayer brings girls closer to God. He can move their hearts and inspire them with hope and guidance. I'm no expert on prayer, but I've seen so many changes in girls when they learn to pray that I have come to have a sobering respect for it. If you feel too timid to pray, or think you don't know how, my advice is just to start. If after reading this book you do this and only this, you will never regret it.

Five: Teach Her about God's Character

The New Testament can be your guide because throughout its pages we read that God was made flesh and showed us directly who He is. He is peace. He is love. He is mercy. He is forgiveness. He is a healer. He is joy. And He is self-sacrifice. We follow Him when we lead lives of love, faith, compassion, and service. And it is about education too—educating ourselves and our families about who God is. You don't need a degree from a seminary to do that. God is available to everyone, not just scholars. Get a copy of the Bible in a translation that works for you—and maybe even read it backwards. Start with the New Testament, which is more accessible, and then read the Old Testament and see how the New Testament is its extraordinary fulfillment.

In my experience, every parent and every daughter needs God, and prayer is the way to find Him. If you give your daughter the gift of faith, you will have given her the greatest gift of all—and the one that will most protect her health and future happiness.

Chapter Nine

Help Her Develop a Healthy Sexuality

From the moment I met Lilly, something about her captured my heart. I don't know if it was her spiraled red hair and freckled face or her shy demeanor. Although I have never met a child I didn't like, there are some in my practice that I would bring home if I could. Lilly was one of those kids. When I finished the physical exam that Lilly needed for second grade, her mother asked me for advice regarding some sleep issues Lilly was having.

Lilly was born the oldest of three girls. Her mother and father divorced when she was eight, shortly after my first visit with her. Her father moved far away, and she never saw him. When I asked about her father, Lilly's mother immediately interrupted, saying, "No, no, no. We don't talk about him. He got in trouble with the law and he left." Then she gave me a somber nod behind Lilly's back conveying that something had gone terribly wrong with him. Lilly was always quiet and reticent, so whenever I asked her direct questions, her mother answered. Many mothers do this either because they are embarrassed that their kids won't talk or because they want to save time. So I didn't think a great deal about it initially.

After that first visit, I saw Lilly every year until she reached her twenty-first birthday. I had a front row seat as she grew up. That's one

141

of the privileges of being a pediatrician. One of the responsibilities is that children confide in me their deepest pains, confusions, and questions.

When Lilly came in for her fifth grade physical, I noticed that she had gained quite a bit of weight. Her mother was puzzled about this, but her daughter didn't seem concerned. Neither mother nor daughter thought there had been any significant changes in Lilly's diet, appetite, or level of exercise. But her mother was worried that Lilly's sleep issues had worsened. After probing a bit, I figured out that Lilly had developed a habit of intense late-night eating. After she finished her homework, she rewarded herself with ice cream, Cheetos, anything that was in the house. I told Lilly that although we shouldn't focus too much on the numbers on the scale (and should focus more on growing up strong in mind and body), late-night binges probably weren't the best thing for her and she'd sleep better without them.

By eighth grade, however, Lilly's weight gain had become a serious issue. When I ask girls about their eating habits, I'm very careful about how I phrase questions because I don't want them to feel insecure or go on extreme diets. Rather than addressing her weight directly, I asked about what was going on in her life. For most kids, excessive weight gain (or weight loss through extreme dieting) is triggered by an underlying emotional issue. Lilly told me that she didn't like going to school anymore because the kids made her uncomfortable with their comments about her appearance and weight, and she was looking forward to being homeschooled.

During this visit, Lilly did most of the talking while her mother sat quietly. But at the end of the exam, Lilly's mother told me that she was struggling as well. Her psychiatrist had recently diagnosed her with bipolar disorder, and she worried about how her condition might have affected Lilly. Then she blurted out, "Dr. Meeker, we think that Lilly is gay." She watched my face to see my reaction.

I didn't comment on that, but I told her that I wanted to see Lilly in six months. To Lilly I said, "I want to follow up on your sleep, your moods, and your schoolwork. Homeschooling is fine, but with your mother working full-time, I don't want you to feel isolated and lonely. So let's check up in six months and see how you're progressing."

Lilly returned six months later, as scheduled. She had lost weight, but I didn't start the discussion there.

"How are things?" I asked.

"Okay, I guess."

"How about your schoolwork, how is that going?"

"Well, like you said, I do spend a lot of time alone now—and I don't like leaving the house. It makes me kind of anxious."

I asked her about friends—didn't she visit them?

"I have a couple of close friends, but they usually come to see me."

"Do you play on a sports team or go out for exercise?"

"No. Like I said, I don't like leaving the house."

Over the course of the next hour in talking to Lilly and her mother, I discovered that Lilly had begun dieting in a very unhealthy way. She had also become more withdrawn, anxious, and depressed, and—to the annoyance of her mother—acted as if she was the de facto parent of her younger sisters.

Then Lilly asked to talk to me privately. She told me that she was worried about her mother's illness, worried about her sisters, worried about her own emotional health, worried about her feelings of loneliness, and worried about her confused sexual orientation.

"I know I'm gay, Dr. Meeker, but the weird thing is, I'm not comfortable talking with girls. I don't chat on social media anymore and only feel comfortable talking to my guy friends. Don't you think this is weird? I mean, what's wrong with me?"

"Let's not worry about that today. Right now, we need to focus on your emotional and physical health."

"I know, but my friends say that if I'm gay, I should talk to girls and, you know, maybe start dating."

"Well, your friends are wrong. You're thirteen years old. You shouldn't be under any pressure to date anyone at all."

At the beginning of her freshman year in high school, Lilly came to see me alone. I barely recognized her. She had shaved one side of her head and dyed the other side pink. But the most striking change was her weight. She had lost a whopping seventy pounds and looked disturbingly thin. When I walked into the exam room, I tried hard to hide my concern and shock. When she saw me, she smiled weakly and proceeded to tell me that her anxiety was worse. But what she really wanted to talk about was being gay. As I asked about her anxiety, she told me that everything would be okay if her friends just accepted her for who she was. She wasn't being bullied, she was rarely on social media, she was still homeschooling, and she rarely left the house, so I had to ask the obvious question.

"Who doesn't accept you?"

"Everyone. If people took me for who I am, things would be so much better. I mean, my mom accepts me, but sometimes my sisters look at me like I'm strange."

"Who else doesn't accept you?"

"Just everyone. I don't see friends that much—really just my closest friends, Mary and Anthony."

"How do they feel about you?"

"Oh, they're cool with me." Then Lilly became quiet.

Whenever I changed the subject to her physical health (her weight loss) or to her emotional health (her depression and anxiety), she rerouted my questions back to her sexuality and reiterated, "If people just accepted me for being gay, then my life would be so much better."

"Well, maybe it would and maybe it wouldn't. Your depression and agoraphobia might not be linked to your sexuality."

She insisted they were, and we left it at that.

I saw Lilly again after she got her driver's license and was planning a road trip to see her father, who lived four hundred miles away. She told me he was married now and had two kids with his new wife. Then she suddenly became pale and refused to make eye contact. I stayed silent.

"Something's wrong, Dr. Meeker, and I'm too embarrassed to talk about it."

I was pretty sure I knew what that something was. But I didn't ask; I waited for her to tell me.

"See, my dad went to jail. Later, he was accused of molesting some kids. We think he was into child porn. At least, that's what my mom said. She doesn't want me to go see him, but I need to. The problem is, I have these incredibly weird feelings."

"Can you describe those feelings?"

"Maybe, but I don't want to."

"You don't need to, but I think if you tell me, you'll feel better."

She sat silently and couldn't seem to get the words out. So I took a chance.

"Lilly, do you have sexual feelings toward your dad?"

She burst into tears and sobbed for a few minutes before saying, "This is sick. *I'm* sick. What is *wrong* with me? I don't even really know him. I barely remember him."

I tried to reassure her that children whose parents were sex offenders sometimes felt this way, and that what she experienced was not a real sexual feeling, but only a distorted desire to be loved by her father.

The good part of that desire went unrewarded because Lilly's road trip to reconnect with her father was a failure. He told her he had no interest in staying in touch with her. In the meantime, her weight stabilized, but she remained confused about her sexuality.

At nineteen, Lilly told me that she thought she might be bisexual.

I asked her if she dated.

"No, not really. I talk to a lot of friends online. I've experimented with women and men a little sexually, but never had any type of real relationship. I just can't seem to trust anyone enough to have a close relationship. You know what I mean?"

"I do know what you mean, Lilly. You've struggled with depression and anxiety, you have a painful, confusing relationship with your father, and you're unsure about your sexuality. But being sexually active won't solve any of those problems, and in fact can make them worse. Put the sex on the back burner. My biggest concern is that you can't get close to someone. I'd like you to focus on that—on developing trust and working on the intimacy that comes from close friendship. You've been so concerned about your sexual identity that you've lost sight of your deeper needs, your deeper self. Friendship will help you discover who are."

Lilly smiled, as if in relief. "Yeah, I guess that makes sense."

Her journey is far from over, but Lilly is starting to find her way— back to her true self, the innocent little girl who had come into my life ten years before.

Development of Healthy Sexuality

In my experience over the past thirty years, Lilly's story is not unusual. We are living in very confusing times for children and adolescents. Our culture has become so fixated on sexualizing children that we have stunted their psychological, sexual, emotional, and mental development. From the time children are in the second grade, they hear about sex, sexual identity, and gender identity. As they move into their preteen years, they learn one overriding sentiment: their sexuality is the most significant part of their identity and defines who they are.

The problem with this is that it's not true. The most important part of our identity is that we are human beings with innate value. Our society's insistence on sexualizing children is obscuring what healthy development is, how complex it is, and how forcing children into making decisions about their "identity" when much of their self-awareness is still in flux too often leads them into unhealthy outcomes.

How Your Daughter Develops Cognitively and Psychologically

Pediatricians and psychologists ranging from Jean Piaget to D. W. Winnicott have outlined the stages of a child's psychological development. When it comes to understanding your daughter, psychoanalyst Erik Erikson's eight stages of development are particularly relevant. Not surprisingly, more than half of the stages—the first five—go from birth through adolescence. The first stage involves a child's sense of basic trust or mistrust, which is strongly linked to maternal affection and care from the time a child is born to the age of two. The second stage, from ages two to four, centers on autonomy versus shame and doubt, where a child learns to do things for herself and gains confidence or fails and is punished, which can lead to a lack of self-esteem. The next stage, from ages four to seven, builds on the last and focuses on successful initiative versus guilt, which the child feels if she senses she is failing to fend for herself. The fourth stage, from ages seven to twelve, is about industry versus inferiority and occurs when a child begins to measure her accomplishments against others' accomplishments (particularly classmates' accomplishments). The fifth stage, which goes from ages twelve to eighteen, is all about identity versus role confusion (which is followed in early mature adulthood with the stage of intimacy versus isolation). The fifth stage is familiar to all parents of teenagers. It is when your child starts branching out to define who she is as an individual who will eventually separate from her parents. All of these stages of development fold into each other, and not only do problems in one stage affect the others, but the process of development involves every aspect of a person—the physical, mental, emotional, and spiritual aspects—and none stands apart from the other. In my medical practice, I have seen over and over again how mind, matter, and spirit are all related. When I see, for instance, the physical results of eating disorders, I know that emotional disorders or depression are almost always behind them.

As daughters mature during adolescence, developmental changes are both more visible and can be more troublesome to kids and parents. During adolescence, your daughter is discovering her whole self. Her knowledge of her feelings, beliefs, personality traits, weaknesses, and limitations is firming up and her intellect is sharpening as her capacity for abstract reasoning grows. She is also going through something of a crisis—realizing that she is part of a family, but also trying to understand what sort of woman she wants to be in the future when she inevitably separates from her family.

Included in all these massive developmental changes going on in your daughter is her concept of her sexual identity. The last thing we should want to do as parents—or as educators, or as a society—is to force our kids to stamp themselves as "gay, straight, bisexual, or transsexual" in early puberty (or even before). We have wrongfully and disproportionately emphasized this aspect of development in ways that can create serious psychological problems for kids.

The brain is highly neuroplastic, or moldable, especially in childhood and adolescence. And considering that a teenager's brain is only 80 percent mature when compared with an adult's brain, there is an enormous opportunity to influence a daughter's beliefs, thoughts, feelings, and identity.

The brilliant psychiatrist Armand Nicholi, who taught at Harvard Medical School and edited *The Harvard Guide to Psychiatry*, told me that sexual identity isn't fully formed until people are in their late teens or early twenties. He believes, as do I, that pressuring teenagers to choose and declare their sexual identity is a tremendous mistake that confuses their natural development.

This does not mean that you should avoid the topic of sex with your teenagers. Not only should you talk to them about sex, but I would say it's a requirement of being a parent. If they don't know your expectations, you should be aware that they certainly know the culture's—which insist that all teenagers are and should be sexually active. Studies show—and it's certainly been my experience—that teenagers are much more likely to postpone sexual activity if they have engaged parents who are willing to have open and honest conversations about sex and sexual development. I know it can be an embarrassing topic for many, but let me guarantee you that after reading this chapter you will have everything you need to have a well-informed, medically correct conversation with your teenagers. (I even have an online program for teens and parents called "How to Have the Talk," which you might find useful.)

A Corrupting Culture

From the magazines they see lining the checkout aisle at the grocery store, to their daily television fare, to the music they listen to (or the music videos they watch), to what their friends post on social media, our daughters are being taught—and they often come to believe—that they must be sexy in order to be significant. They're also told that sexual activity must be the most important and exciting aspect of anyone's life.

The result is plummeting self-esteem because they can't be as beautiful as the models on Instagram or the ones they see in magazines. They are far too young for sexual activity, and if they do engage in sexual activity, the results are almost uniformly traumatizing. Girls need love, commitment, and the true intimacy that comes from deep friendship. But our sexualized culture separates sex from these three essentials.

The fact is that our culture is seriously misguided on sex. Many adults, for instance, erroneously believe that "most kids" have sex in high school, but studies don't bear that out. According to the Centers for Disease Control and Prevention, sexually active teens are in the minority (around 40 percent)[1]—and that number would surely be lower if there weren't so many low expectations and cultural pressure for teenagers to be sexually active.

I have repeatedly had girls who are my patients tell me how pressured they are to be sexually active in high school. One young girl who was a virgin before her senior prom told me several weeks after it that she had sex with her boyfriend because she "just couldn't take the pressure anymore." Her peers told her that if she wanted to keep her boyfriend, she had to have sex with him. Finally, she did it—and regretted it. He broke up with her anyway, and she told me that having had sex with him made the breakup much harder for her.

A healthy sexual culture would be one that teaches teens about the benefits of deferring sexual activity, the beauty of sex within marriage, and the fact that sex is about bonding couples together and creating a family. That shouldn't be so hard to understand. But our culture seems intent on making sex become something else entirely—a sort of competition (who can be the sexiest), a statement of our identity, and a matter of personal fulfillment.

The Role of Parents

Parents can help a lot here. If you are open to talking with your daughter about sex, not only can you teach her the reasons to defer sexual activity, but you also can support her when she is confronted by peer pressure. You can let her know that becoming sexually active won't increase a boy's commitment to her (in fact, it will almost certainly lessen it) and that most teens do not engage in sexual activity. Even today, deferring sexual activity is normal, not to mention safer—physically, mentally, and emotionally—for young people.

The family atmosphere you provide for your daughters affects them in ways that might surprise you. For instance, girls who have a father in the home generally start their periods later than girls who don't. Less surprising might be the fact that girls with supportive, loving parents are far less likely to become involved in drugs or underage drinking, or to suffer from anxiety or depression, or to become sexually active in their teen years. They also are far more likely to do well in school. Sadly, girls who come from troubled homes and suffered from sexual abuse have far higher rates of depression, anxiety, behavioral issues, and problems with their sexual identity. This is because a girl's sexuality connects with her ability to trust and love, with intimacy, and with her feelings of self-respect and self-control.

Inevitably, what a daughter's family thinks about sex strongly influences her own views. Many parents believe that if they encourage their daughters to postpone sex until they are married, then their daughters will rebel and become promiscuous. This is absolutely not true; in fact, the opposite is true. If you teach your daughter that sex is so important (and in the right context, wonderful) that it should be deferred until she is older or married, she will feel that you respect her and care deeply about her future. The trick is not to teach your daughter that sex is shameful or wrong. That is the attitude that can inspire rebellion. You should teach her that sex is something to be cherished, something to be saved for the right time in your daughter's life.

Girls and Sex: What You Need to Know

About a dozen years ago, I wrote a popular book called *Strong Fathers, Strong Daughters*. Fathers, who otherwise loved the book, told me that they hated the chapter on sex. It wasn't just that the subject made them uncomfortable; it was that the data I revealed on the dangers of teen sex were frightening. My response is this: parents need to know the truth so that they can educate their kids. The dangers surrounding teenage sexual activity are even worse now than they were then. The fact is that we are living through an epidemic of sexually transmitted diseases and infections. The data is out there for anyone with eyes to see—you can look for yourself at the Centers for Disease Control and Prevention website or at medinstitute.org—but it goes virtually unacknowledged and unreported. Here are some the numbers you should know about:

- Every year in the United States, there are twenty million new cases of sexually transmitted diseases.[2]
- Half of these cases involve teens and young adults between the ages of fifteen and twenty-five, although they make up just over a quarter of the population.[3]
- Studies show that one in four young women has a sexually transmitted disease.[4]
- More than more 80 percent of sexually active women will be infected with HPV (human papilloma virus) at one point or another.[5]
- High risk strains of HPV cause cervical, anal, oropharyngeal, vaginal, and vulvar cancer. Ninety-one percent of cervical cancer is caused by HPV, and sexually active teenage girls are the ones most at risk.[6]
- Chlamydia is the most common sexually transmitted disease in the United States. Most infections occur in women under the age of twenty-five.[7]

- Since 2009, the rate of reported cases of gonorrhea has increased by 75.2 percent.[8]
- Sexually transmitted diseases are the second most common reason for women to have fertility problems.[9]
- Some sexually transmitted diseases do not show immediate symptoms, so patients might not know they have them or seek treatment.[10]
- Having a sexually transmitted disease (specifically HIV) is the leading cause of death in women of reproductive age worldwide.[11]

Looking at these statistics is unnerving and even hard to believe—and that is part of the problem: few people want to believe it. Much of popular culture is dedicated to denying it, and many parents, teachers, and physicians feel inadequate to deal with it.

Beyond these already alarming statistics lie other serious dangers for teenagers and young adult girls who are sexually active. Our go-to cure for these problems is contraception, but contraception will not prevent girls from being pressured into sex. It can even increase the pressure because it allows "safe sex"—only it doesn't, neither physically nor psychologically. Contraception will neither protect girls from sexual violence nor fully protect them from sexually transmitted diseases. Most girls don't risk death with a pregnancy, but they can risk it with any number of sexually transmitted infections. What most girls really need is not more access to contraception, but dating advice—especially about setting rules and boundaries. But parents become reluctant to give this over time.

When girls reach college age, most parents have pretty much accepted that their daughters will be sexually active and assume that this is both fine and a healthy part of growing up—as long as their boyfriends use condoms, which will protect their daughters from unwanted pregnancies and sexually transmitted diseases.

The problem is that while condoms offer some protection, young people often don't use them consistently. This is partly because of their natural feelings of invincibility—an unplanned pregnancy or sexual disease "will never happen to me," they think—and partly because sexually active young people can become jaded and don't really care about themselves. They become complacent, even numb, after many sexual encounters, and their sexual activity is often fueled by alcohol or drugs. This is especially true with girls who participate in the "hook-up" culture—where they have sex with someone and then never see them again—or if they see college as a time to experiment sexually with women and men. One study showed that two-thirds of college students have had "friends with benefits."[12] Many see casual sex as an expression of "progressive" beliefs. Many girls also believe that they can have sex without emotional or psychological repercussions, but the truth is that this is impossible neurophysiologically.

About a decade ago, Dr. Joe McIlhaney and Dr. Freda McKissic Bush wrote an eye-opening book called *Hooked: New Science on How Casual Sex Is Affecting Our Children*, which laid out in accessible details how sexual activity creates dramatic chemical changes in the brain.[13] Every parent of a high school or college student should read it. McIlhaney is an obstetrician-gynecologist and served on the Research Task Force in the National Campaign to Prevent Teen Pregnancy. He started the Medical Institute for Sexual Health and has overseen the publication of the best medical research available on teen sex. Bush currently heads the Medical Institute for Sexual Health.

They describe in their book how a girl's brain releases oxytocin during sexual activity. Oxytocin is a hormone that promotes human bonding—both between the girl and her partner, and between a mother and her newborn. Even if a girl thinks she is engaging in casual sex, her brain is telling her otherwise—that her sexual partner is someone with whom she has a profound bond. A girl's brain chemistry acts as though sexual intercourse should be part of a long-term relationship. If she breaks that bond, and if that long-term relationship does not exist, then she will suffer psychological or emotional effects, which is why depression in girls is so often linked to premature sexual activity.

Girls, Their Feelings, and Sex

"I just don't know what's wrong" Margo's mother said. "Last year, tenth grade seemed so easy for her. She had good friends, her grades were good, and dance was going really well."

Margo and her mother had always had a great relationship, so when Margo asked if she could speak with me privately and her mother agreed to leave the room, I knew something was seriously wrong.

Margo told me that she had been feeling sad, lonely, and depressed. I asked how long this had been going on.

"Well, I think it came on slowly. Last summer, I felt pretty good. But after school started in the fall, I just wasn't into it. I mean, school's not really my thing anyway, but I never minded it as much as I did last fall."

I waited awhile, and she continued.

"I just don't get it. Now I don't want to be around my friends. They think I'm a snob now, and I don't know what to tell them. I just want to be home alone."

Margo had been my patient for years. I'd never seen her melancholy before, and I'd never seen her look this way. Margo had always had an eye for clothes and taken care of herself and taken a polite pride in her appearance. But today she looked unkempt.

"Are you sleeping okay?" I asked.

"Yeah. If anything, I sleep too much. But I have to because I'm always tired. I've missed a lot of days at school because I just feel too tired to go. I think I have mono."

"Maybe," I said. "Tell me, are you getting along well with your mom and dad?"

"Yeah. I mean, we don't argue or anything. My mom and I are close, and we always have been."

"What about your friends? Have you had any falling outs with any of them?"

"No. Not really. Like I said, I just don't see them as much as I used to."

"Sorry, Margo, but I need to ask: Are you using any drugs, drinking?"

"Nope," she said with her head bowed to the floor.

"What about any other changes? Did anyone you know die? Have you had any boyfriends, close friends leave?"

She looked up at me and she looked surprised. "Yeah. I had a boyfriend last summer. I really liked him, but he lives downstate, so we don't see each other anymore. We broke up at the end of the summer because it was silly trying to have a long-distance relationship. It was hard because I really liked him."

"Were you two having sex?"

"Well, yeah. Of course. That's what all kids my age do—particularly if you really like someone."

"Margo, I know you've dated other guys. Did you have sex with them too?"

"Sure."

"I don't remember you telling me this. I've known you for a long time."

"I know. I was just embarrassed to say anything. I didn't want my mom to know because she would be upset."

I talked with Margo for another twenty minutes, and it became clear that her depression began shortly after she broke-up with her boyfriend and worsened in the ensuing months. Margo told me that although she liked him, she wasn't that serious about him because she knew he might not want a long-term relationship. Nevertheless, they had been sexually active together all summer. She wasn't sexually active because she wanted to be—she didn't particularly like it or dislike it—but because "it was what he expected." What she didn't expect was the depression that followed.

In my experience and as studies confirm, Margo's situation is common. Many girls who have been sexually active, particularly after many sexual partners, suffer some level of depression. Interestingly, they don't associate their feelings with sex because they regard sexual activity as healthy, which of course it can be under the right circumstances—but not when it severs the bond between sexual intercourse and commitment.

When a sexual relationship ends, a girl suffers from that lack of commitment and loses some sense of value, trust, affection, and intimacy—all of which can lead to depression. Girls in this situation have a hard time recognizing the cause of their depression because they think sexual activity is empowering and makes them more mature. On the one hand, they will tell me that sex is a tremendous physical, emotional, and even spiritual experience; and on the other hand, they will say—as Margo did—that it's really no big deal and you can do it with anyone you like. Their depression lies within that contradiction. To her brain, emotions, and body, sexual activity is a big deal.

Depression is a very serious problem for teens and has risen so dramatically[14] that primary care physicians are often on the front line of treating it. But the best treatment of course is prevention—and that means teaching our kids the truth about sex, which is something that we as a culture have been very bad at for decades.

How Every Parent Can Make a Difference

When it comes to teaching a daughter about her sexuality, sexual development, or sexual activity, most parents feel insecure. We either feel embarrassed or inadequate. The truth is that parents have more influence over a daughter's view of her sexuality and the decisions she makes about sex than any friend or boyfriend. There are some practical things that any parent can do.

When she is young, teach your daughter to have "body boundaries." From the time a girl is about three or four years old, she can learn that the body parts covered by a bathing suit are private. I tell my girl patients of this age that their bodies are beautiful and need special care, and that there are parts that only a doctor or her parents should see. The important thing at this stage is to set boundaries, help your daughter feel good about herself, and encourage a sense of self-protection. The focus should not be on shame, but on pride.

Teach her that her value comes from being a young woman, not from some expression of her sexuality. One of the biggest harms our culture is doing to our children is confronting them with the mechanics of sexuality, asking them to make sexual choices, and treating them as sexually active far too young. Children respond well to and can understand valuing other people as *human beings,* and that should be our focus rather than saying that they should respect a wide variety of sexual choices—which for many children is extremely confusing, upsetting, and can lead to unhealthy behaviors (such as dangerous promiscuity passing itself off as harmless experimentation).

From an early age, talk to your daughter about deep subjects and keep the conversations going as she gets older. If your daughter is used to talking about important topics with you, having "the talk" will be much easier later on. Ideally, it will be an ongoing conversation that will allow you to have more influence on her decision-making. Open and honest communication at age-appropriate levels will do more to enhance your relationship with your daughter than almost anything else.

Pay attention to what her classmates are talking about. It is much healthier for a girl to hear about sex from a parent than from a peer. Your daughter *wants* your guidance, so be ready to offer it when she's ready—and before her peers do. The best way to know when your daughter is ready is when she comes to you with questions. If she asks once and then runs off to play, you can defer the subject. But if she repeats her questions and acts genuinely interested, it's time.

Establish yourself as the "go-to" person when it comes to information about sex, dating, body changes, or anything personal. Every person has a built-in modesty about sex. Our culture tries to break that modesty down, but we need to preserve it and help our daughters preserve it as well. One way you can help her preserve that modesty is by encouraging her to come to you when she has questions about sensitive topics like sex. However awkward the topic, be honest with her. It will underline her belief that you (and not her peers) have the correct answers and that you are the one who can discuss sex in its proper context of love, respect, and commitment. Don't *assume* that your daughter fully understands your opinions and beliefs; make *certain* that she knows.

Remember that mom and dad have different teaching roles. A mother has an obvious, powerful influence over her daughter. A daughter is more likely to talk to her mother—and her mother obviously sets the standard for femininity and all the good that comes with it. Be sure to use that power wisely. Be her guide in kindness, compassion, and morality, and she will likely follow in your footsteps. Mothers typically have a far easier time than dads in recognizing how they can guide their daughters. But make no mistake—dads set the standard for what their daughters should expect from a man. Daughters who receive affection, respect, and acceptance from their fathers are far less likely to become prematurely sexually active, and they have a sense of security and self-worth that doesn't require affirmation from sexually aggressive boyfriends. When your daughter dates someone, she will subconsciously compare her date with you, her father, and she will wonder what you would think of him. If you avoid foul language, she will likely disdain men who don't. If you are respectful, she will likely reject men who aren't. If you are morally strong, she will likely avoid men who are morally weak. But the reverse is true too. If a girl's father was abusive, she will more likely accept an abusive boyfriend. Family patterns often repeat themselves.

Stay engaged. Many parents have an initial talk with their daughters about sex and then let the subject go, believing that their work is done. This is far from true. When your daughter is in fourth grade, sixth grade, and on through high school and even college, it is critical to talk to her about what you hope for and expect from her. Often the best way to initiate conversations on delicate subjects is to ask what her friends are up to—if they are dating, adjusting well to school, or working on special projects. Show sincere interest and don't pass judgment. Your real goal is to get a glimpse into what *she* is thinking and doing. Once you have that, you can more easily guide the conversation back to where she is in life.

Make sure she doesn't feel pressured by anyone about sex or her sexuality. We all know the dangers of peer pressure when it comes to girls becoming sexually active, but today girls also feel extraordinary pressure from friends, the media, and teachers to stamp themselves as gay, straight, bisexual, or transgender. Don't let her feel that pressure. Give her time to figure things out about herself—and to ask you when she needs help.

Set high standards for her. By the time she's in high school, if not before, popular culture will try to inculcate in your daughter the idea that her value depends on her being sexy. Tell her the truth: that the media see sex as a tool to sell things and make money, and that she shouldn't let herself be manipulated for their benefit. Girls are smart, and if you tell her this, she'll most likely see the truth in it and reject the media's message. Teach her that sex is about love and commitment, and for that reason (and for every medical reason you can imagine) she should think in terms of having one lifetime sexual partner: her future husband. Tell her that you are setting this high standard not because sex is bad, but because it will guarantee her the most satisfying and healthiest sex life for decades to come and maximize her potential for being a healthy mother. I know this sounds prudish to many parents today, but it is a simple fact of life that is reflected in every statistic you can find about sexually transmitted diseases, depression, and infertility.

Be a good role model. Many single parents who are dating or have live-in boyfriends or girlfriends tell their daughters to do what they say, not what they do. But kids see right through this. If you're having sex and you aren't married, she will too. But her problem is that because of her age, she is at a higher risk for sexually transmitted diseases and depression than you are. So be a good parent; set a good example.

I know that most parents are frightened for their daughters—and they should be—but they also capitulate far too easily to what they assume "all teenagers do" and rely, as they shouldn't, on sex education classes at school. These programs are often medically inaccurate and have no positive record of making a difference in changing teen sexual behaviors (except perhaps for the worse).

A far better way to teach her is to stay connected with your daughter, to communicate your own beliefs and standards, and to encourage her to come to you when she has questions. She is the child and you are the grownup (and she will feel this way even when she's forty). So stay connected, support her, and don't be afraid to set high expectations.

Chapter Ten

Help Her Find Good Friends (and Deal with the Bad Ones)

"**D**r. Meeker," Lacey started, "you just don't get it. When I'm around certain people I get so anxious. It's kind of like my heart wants to jump out of my chest. I never used to feel this way. But now, sometimes I get so scared that I don't want to leave the house."

Her friend Chelsea piped in, saying, "She's right, you know. I've seen her get this way. I mean, one second we'll be talking in the hall, and suddenly she'll say, 'Chelsea, I've got to get out of here.' The problem is, I don't know what to do. What should I do?"

They looked at me with pleading stares, hoping I had an answer.

First, I had a question: "Lacey, where's your mother? It's a bit unusual to come in with a friend and not a parent."

"Oh, my mom couldn't come. She's at work. She really wanted to be here, but it's okay. I told her that Chelsea could drive me. Plus Chelsea knows everything about me. We've been friends since I was in third grade."

Chelsea said, "We're really close, Dr. Meeker—like sisters. We don't have any secrets from each other. When my parents got divorced last year, Lacey was there for me. It was really tough: my mom just cried all the time, my dad wanted full custody of me, and I just wanted to get away. Lacey's mom let me stay with them for a few months so I could get some peace. They saved my life."

I believed it. I've seen this a lot with teenage girls who are close friends and support each other with incredible maturity, as these two girls did—especially when parents get divorced or are otherwise disengaged (usually because of work).

Lacey felt stressed about school, her ability to get into college, and her father's approval (which she felt was, in part, conditional on her academic success). She had panic attacks. She felt stressed more often than a normal teenager should. In fact, she suffered from acute anxiety. I see a lot more cases like Lacey's than I did fifteen years ago. Today, nearly a third of teenagers—and 38 percent of teenage girls—have symptoms like Lacey's.[1]

Lacey worked diligently with me and with professional counselors to overcome her anxiety—and she did, in no small part thanks to the support of her Chelsea. The summer before Lacey went to college, her anxiety was well under control, but she felt guilty about leaving Chelsea, who was a grade behind her in school.

"I know this sounds silly," she said that summer, "but I don't worry about my mom or dad. They've gotten used to the idea that I'm leaving. But Chelsea and me? Not so much."

I saw Lacey again during her Christmas break—and not only was college going well, but so was her friendship with Chelsea. "We'll always be there for each other," she said. She meant it, and I knew she was right.

Why Our Girls Need Friendships

Many of us as parents assume our daughter's friendships are fleeting and even insignificant. But they aren't. As adults, we put friendships in the perspective of a long and varied life. But our daughters don't have that perspective. For them, friendships are new and powerful and can lead to elation or despair because they are experiencing the intense feelings of love and acceptance (as well as judgment and rejection) that come from friendship for the first time. When girls make close friends, their emotional world rapidly expands through shared secrets, thoughts, and feelings. Friendship is your daughter's first important relationship outside the home. This can be both thrilling and terrifying for her—and it propels her into more friendships.

I still remember the kinship I felt with my best friend in the third grade. My teacher had reprimanded me because I wore shorts beneath my skirt. I did that so I could run and tumble and not have to worry. But my teacher said it was wholly unfeminine and no other girl did it—except for one. I quickly learned her name, and the bond we formed—which started in stubborn rebellion—grew into a close, fun friendship.

My best friend in the sixth grade was Sandy. We rode horses together for hours upon hours in the woods outside Boston. As we trotted through those beautiful woods, we talked about life, how much she missed her father (her parents had divorced), our shared interests (especially horses), and our fears. She helped me become a better rider, and I helped her come to grips with her parents' divorce. I always thought she was amazing. I think in some ways we both felt sorry for each other. I felt sorry for the hurt she endured from her parents' divorce while I had a secure and happy home life, and I think she felt a little sorry for me because she was by far the better horsewoman and the better student. We even went to college near one another. She went to Smith College and I went to Mount Holyoke College in Massachusetts, and we continued to ride together and share our academic and personal successes and failures.

Early friendships like these shape us more powerfully than later friendships because we're still discovering who we are when we're young. By the time we reach adulthood, we've had enough experience to know ourselves, and while our friendships can be very close, they are unlikely to be as formative as early friendships.

Girls Long for Deep Connection and Joy

Girls are emotionally complex, and if there is one thing that defines them, it is confusion about their feelings. Girls gravitate toward people who can help them understand their feelings. Especially if a girl has gone through a trauma—if her parents divorced or if one of them dies—she might feel isolated or she might withdraw, and she will need a friend to help her make sense of what has happened. This is true also for girls going through the physical and emotional changes of adolescence.

Finding one or two very close friends who can offer support and understanding is very important to girls. One close friend can give a girl hope, improve her self-esteem, keep her from falling into depression, and help her navigate mild or moderately painful events.

Celia did this for Theresa.

When Theresa was in sixth grade, she started at a new school. She had moved from California to Michigan and was upset about the move. She had good friends in California and cried about leaving them behind. Her mother reassured her that she would still stay close with them because there were ample opportunities through Skype and Facebook. But Theresa knew better. Even at age twelve, she fully understood that the Internet was no substitute for spending real time with her friends.

She was also anxious because she was starting junior high school. This is always a tumultuous time, and she rightly anticipated that she would have an even harder school year because she knew no one.

At five feet eight, she was the tallest girl in her class. Not only was she self-conscious about her height, but she also worried about her weight. She was gangly and thin, and in her first week at school a girl named Jessica made fun of her, saying that she "looked like a giraffe with no body." Celia overheard the comment. She knew what it was like to be the new girl because she had moved into the area only a year earlier. Self-confident and compassionate, she sat by Theresa at lunch. After getting to know her a little, she said, "I overheard Jessica's giraffe comment. Don't let her bother you. She does that to everybody. No one pays attention. She says mean things, but if you ignore her, she'll stop and she might even become your friend. She's weird that way."

Theresa immediately felt relief and was grateful for Celia's advice. Over the following weeks, the two girls became very good friends, and sure enough—Jessica stopped her mean comments. Sixth grade brought other issues for Theresa, and when they arose she immediately turned to Celia. It seemed that Celia always understood. Theresa told me, "I don't know what it is about her, but we just 'get' each other. I know it sounds like I'm always the one having issues, but it really isn't that way. She moved to Michigan a year earlier than I did and she still really misses the friends she left behind. When she feels lonely, we get together and cheer each other up." Their friendship grew through high school. It helped them get through all the inevitable trials of teenage life. No matter the circumstances, they knew they could always share their thoughts and feelings with each other and support each other. Reciprocal friendships are healthy friendships, and our daughters need them.

Friends Help Girls Understand Themselves Better

Many girls see their reflection in their friends to the point of adopting a friend's mannerisms and characteristics. Close friends help girls define their identities apart from their families, which is why *good* friendships are so important and why bad ones can be so damaging.

When a girl struggles with self-confidence and becomes friends with a girl who has more self-confidence, her self-esteem climbs. She sees how a confident peer acts, talks, and feels. Then she tells herself that it may be okay if she imitates that friend. Research clearly shows that having a healthy friendship improves many aspects of a girl's life, and self-esteem is one of them. Interestingly, having a single close friendship is more important than having a group of friends.

New research published in *Child Development* shows that teens aged fifteen and sixteen who had one close friend, rather than a bigger peer group featuring less intense relationships, reported higher levels of self-worth and lower levels of social anxiety and depression at age twenty-five when compared with their peers who were more broadly popular as teens.[2]

In fact, another study confirmed that when a girl was affiliated with a broader group of friends, she was more likely to suffer from anxiety as she got older. The authors concluded that girls who prioritize forming close friendships are better able to manage social and developmental tasks as they move into adulthood than girls who try to fit into a large group of peers.[3]

This is an important point for parents. We often preach to our daughters that they need to expand their group of friends or get involved in more activities. We do this because we want our daughters to be popular and well-accepted. What we fail to realize, however, is that having a large group of friends is stressful for some girls and can make them more vulnerable to peer pressure and bullying. Having a few good friends can be much better for a girl than having more friends who are less close, and perhaps less kind and less supportive. All of us are influenced by the habits of our friends. For instance, if your best friend eats healthily, you are five times more likely to have a healthy diet yourself.[4] But our young, emotionally developing daughters are especially malleable with their friendships, which is why the quality of their friendships—not the quantity—is what is most important. (Although for fully formed adults, having more friends can be a good thing to stay socially active and have a broader network of support.)

Parents often ask me how they can help their daughters make more friends. Most of the girls are shy and have one or two close friends, and their parents will tell me, "All she wants to do is come home and read, listen to music, or work on a project by herself. How can we bring her out of her shell?"

The answer is that maybe you shouldn't. There is nothing abnormal in this behavior; it is simply a personality type. Girls who are natural introverts are perfectly comfortable with a good friend or two, enjoy being alone, and are perfectly well-adjusted. Parents often fear that their daughters will feel rejected or like outcasts, or will suffer from low self-esteem, loneliness, or anxiety if they aren't part of a larger group of friends. But the truth is that most girls in this situation feel perfectly fine and are at less emotional risk than if they were in conscious pursuit of popularity. If your daughter is shy and introverted but has a few close friends and seems perfectly content, it's probably not a problem.

Close friendships help daughters grow emotionally. They learn how to deal with conflict, they learn how to be assertive, they learn more about their own personalities, and they use friendships to fulfill personal needs. That's natural, and it's why, to some degree, "opposites attract." For instance, girls who are needy tend to befriend girls who need to help others. Girls who are confrontational are often attracted to quiet, unassuming girls who can balance their mood swings.

Interestingly, girls who are secure and self-confident generally make friends with other secure and self-confident girls. Why? Because they tend to be more mature, so they need less support and can engage in more adult-level friendships. On the other hand, less-secure girls will sometimes seek friends in order to gain status—and these friendships are almost invariably tenuous and unfulfilling. There are many subconscious reasons that girls become friends, but astute parents can usually figure out the dynamics of their daughters' friendships pretty quickly and advise them on appropriate ways to interact.

Friends Help Them to Be Happier

Numerous studies about women and girls have shown that close friendships lead to greater happiness. A landmark study done at UCLA found that friendship actually changes brain chemistry.[5] The study concluded that the more friends women had, the less likely they were to develop physical impairments as they aged and the more likely they were to be leading joyful lives. In fact, the results were so significant that the researchers warned that not having close friends or confidants was as detrimental to your health as smoking or carrying extra weight. The study dove deeper into why this would be. It turns out that friendships play a big part in lowering stress in women, which leads to increased happiness. Women who share their lives with close friends have higher levels of the neurohormone oxytocin (which reduces stress), have lower blood pressure, and live healthier and longer.

Although this study was done on women, it has important ramifications for our daughters. We know, for instance, that girls have oxytocin in their cerebrospinal fluid that influences their moods. Many young girls experience stress, and there is no reason to think that their neuro-chemicals respond differently to stress than women's do. And the studies done on women show the effects of friendship over time; many of those friendships may have started when they were young. While there are some differences between women's and girls' friendships, there are many qualities that are the same.

Different Types of Friendship

It is important to understand why our daughters form certain friend-ships because we can then help them navigate those friendships. Some are healthy and others can be toxic. The reasons girls fall into one or the other can reveal a lot about how they view themselves.

The great philosopher Aristotle wrote about three fundamental reasons for friendship in his *Nicomachean Ethics*. The first is seeking a friend for utility—in other words, to get something from that friend. Business relationships might fall in this category. The second is to enjoy pleasure—the pleasure of a friend's companionship, perhaps in the pur-suit of common interests or hobbies. The third and highest and rarest reason for friendship is the pursuit of virtue, where both parties are mature, well-balanced, live good lives, and come together with the pur-pose of recognizing, guiding, and helping each other toward virtue.

Usually our daughters find friends that serve a purpose—generally an emotional one—as a means to find happiness, peace, empathy, or compassion. The true value—and likely length—of a friendship is based on how reciprocal it is. If it is truly based on shared care and respect, then the relationship will blossom and strengthen each girl. There are some friendships, however, that are not healthy and should be discouraged.

The Drama Queen

We all know women and girls like this. They are the ones who exag-gerate every ailment or bad encounter. They see themselves as having unique experiences that no one else has ever had. Sometimes they over-state happy situations, but usually they focus on the negative. The pur-pose of their drama is to garner attention, and even sympathy. Friends may respond at first, but most will quickly tire of the drama, feel they are being manipulated, and back away.

Adults know the type, but girls may not recognize that they're being manipulated. That's the problem with manipulation—it sometimes works. The dominant friend knows exactly how to maneuver the other person in order to feel more powerful. She gains what she "needs" because she has learned her friend's personality well enough to arouse sympathy, anger, or whatever other emotion she is trying to elicit.

The Drainer

This is a "friend" who drains her listener by constantly talking about her woes and has no interest in what is going on in the listening friend's life. The relationship is profoundly one-sided.

The girl upon whom the drainer dumps all her woes at first feels as though she is being a very good friend. After all, she is told, her capacity to care and listen is like no other. Although this feels flattering at first, over time the listener becomes emotionally exhausted and realizes that no matter how often she is praised for being a good listener, the friend-ship is not reciprocal. The drainer is using her and leaving her with nothing but fatigue and a feeling of guilt if she tries to extricate herself from this unhealthy relationship.

The Broken-Winged Friend

This is the girl who needs fixing—and convinces her friend/victim that *only* she can fix her. The broken-winged girl may have gone through genuine trauma or, more likely, she will exaggerate her woes in order to gain sympathy.

The real harm in this relationship comes from the ever-increasing demands of the broken-winged girl on her friend who can never give enough of her time (especially her time with other friends). The healer inevitably ends up angry and bitter, because although the broken-winged friend will praise her help, the healer understandably wonders, "If I am doing her such good, why do I feel so bad about it?" And she is absolutely right—she can't feel good about it because what has developed is an unhealthy, codependent relationship that needs to stop.

The Edgy Friend

Just as girls can be attracted to "bad" boys, so too can they be attracted to "bad girls." A straight-laced girl may think a promiscuous girl is cooler, or more popular, or more self-confident, or living a more thrilling life than her own and want to share some of that excitement. Of course, this is a bad misreading of the situation and a terrible mistake, but many young girls are simply too immature to understand this (or think they don't care, which is part of the same problem).

The edgy friend invariably leads the naïve one into trouble, usually with the promise that if she changes her life, she'll live more authentically and be happier—which can lead to promiscuity, taking drugs, smoking, abusing alcohol, and even getting into trouble with the law. The naïve girl does these things to impress the edgy friend and fit in with her crowd—and, even more importantly, to get attention from those outside the crowd, including her parents. Boys who join gangs often do so in order to win admiration and attention and be part of a pack. Girls will join an edgy crowd for similar reasons. There is nothing wrong with these needs or desires, but in both cases they are being pursued in destructive ways.

The Idolizer

Many girls who have success in an area—athletics, academics, or the arts—or whose parents are successful will have girls who sidle up to them because of that success. These idolizing girls want to be close to a successful person because it makes them feel more important. The problem is that because the idolizer always feels inferior, true friendship can't exist.

Successful girls often learn to be wary of other girls offering friendship because they will have learned from experience that while attention and accolades are nice, any friendship not based on who she is (rather than what she has done) will never last because it is not authentic. Friendship with an idolizer leaves both girls feeling used and awkward; the successful girl feels used for her status, and the idolizer will eventually find the inequality of the relationship unsatisfying.

The Mean Girls

Then, of course, there are the mean girls—the ones who make everyone else's life miserable. They manipulate people, pit one girl (or group of girls) against another, bully, lie, and seemingly enjoy disrupting healthy relationships. They are such a well-known type that movies have been made about them, and parents naturally fear that the mean girls might prey on their daughters.

Parents are right to be vigilant about bullying, but there is no reason to be paranoid about the mean girls or to exaggerate their influence. Yes, mean girls can hurt others and make their lives miserable *for a time*, but with the right parenting, their impact can be minimal.

Caroline met Diane on her first day of third grade. Diane, a recent arrival from out-of-state, seemed glamorous, dressed in trendy clothes, and was widely envied by all the other girls for her style.

Diane gathered four or five girls—Caroline among them—into her clique. She hosted parties at her house. She watched PG-13 movies when her mom was around and R-rated movies when she wasn't and enjoyed shocking her friends.

Around Christmas, Diane told her friends via Instagram that Caroline should no longer be part of the group—she was failing math, she was stupid, and she even smelled bad. Caroline was beside herself. How could Diane do this to her? She had been Diane's first friend at the new school and had helped her acclimate. Now the other girls in the clique shunned her. Caroline's mother noticed that something was wrong because Caroline became withdrawn and prone to tears, and quickly figured out that Diane and her clique must have turned against her.

So her mother had Caroline invite *other* friends from her class over to their home. She offered to take them to amusement parks, shopping, and out to lunch. Occasionally, a girl would accept the invitation, but most of the time Caroline and her mother were turned down because Diane's influence over her peers was that strong.

Caroline's mother then decided to have a talk with her daughter about meanness and mean girls. She didn't try to minimize Caroline's hurt feelings, but she also taught her over the course of the next few months that she could control her feelings, resolve her hurt (understanding that Diane's hostility was likely the result of some deep insecurity), and move on. Her mother also succeeded in encouraging Caroline to get closer with friends outside of school—friends from her chorale group and dance troupe. That worked over time, and Caroline and a new friend formed a close bond.

Mean girls come in all shapes, sizes, and ethnic and religious backgrounds. Some are born with challenging personalities and others are wounded into it. You can keep tabs on the social dynamics of your daughter's friends, but usually the ups and downs of friendship don't require parental involvement. And don't be so worried about bullying that you teach her that she should *expect* to be bullied, because anticipation can lead to overreaction. Also remember that there are different levels of offense. If in first grade a mean girl pulls your daughter's pigtails when no one is looking—that's for her to handle. If she's a teenager and a mean girl or a mean group of girls calls your daughter a slut, perhaps on social media, then you need to intervene immediately and aggressively. If the incident happened at school, then you must speak with the teacher. If she doesn't act, then you go to the principle. If she does nothing, then you go to the abuser's parents with proof in hand and talk with the bully's parents without the girls present. If the child's parents refuse a meeting, then you have to weigh whether the bully did something illegal. If so, you need to report it to the police. Anti-bullying laws exist in every state to protect the innocent and deter bad behavior.

We need to stop bullies from throwing our girls into despair. Today the bullies often operate on social media, which they assume is out of bounds for parents. Once they realize that parents—and even law enforcement officials—are paying attention, their behavior will change.

When you tell your daughter that you will see everything she sends and receives on social media, she will have a fit. She may yell, scream, slam doors, and call you a terrible parent. Oh well. She is a kid (even if she's seventeen) who has no idea how to handle cruelty and slander. You do. So be there. Don't back down, do your job as a parent, and limit the risk that your daughter will experience harmful comments or photos.

Why Girls Hurt Other Girls

When a daughter comes home crying because a friend rejected her or did something mean, most of us are quick to tell her that she doesn't deserve to be treated this way or that the person who hurt her is a jerk. That's true, of course, but if we can provide an explanation for why the mean girl behaved the way she did, it will help our daughter make better sense of it, and thus recover from her hurt more quickly.

Jealousy

The overwhelming majority of girls who hurt others do so because they are jealous of them. A girl may feel threatened by another's figure, attractiveness, popularity, talents, intelligence, or a hundred other things. Jealousy is one of the most toxic feelings a human being can have, and when it rests in the heart of an immature, self-centered girl, trouble appears. A girl's knee-jerk reaction to jealousy is to strike at the revered target—and social media platforms have made it easier than ever to lash out at someone else.

Jealousy might seem like a difficult concept to explain, but it's not really, as we can see in fairy tales like Snow White and Cinderella. Insecure girls might express dislike for your daughter because she is pretty and composed ("little Miss Perfect"), or religious and virtuous ("little Miss Goody Two-Shoes"), or smart ("little Miss Nerd"), or a great athlete ("little Miss Jock").

Your daughter likely won't want to hear bad things about her former friend—or at the other extreme, she might be incensed into wanting revenge—but you can help her find understanding by asking her if she has ever wanted to be like someone else or have something that someone else had. Once you get her to tap into her own feelings, then you can tell her that this is what the offender feels times ten. Jealousy makes people, even good people, do cruel things. It never has anything to do with the target; it always reflects the heart of the offender. Over time, even a young girl can understand this and take it to heart.

Insecurity

In many ways, we parents do a disservice to our kids by constantly telling them how great they are. We encourage them to find their passion, to use their talents, and to be the best. These are good and well-intentioned encouragements. But when we go overboard, we can lead our kids into a trap, thinking that because they are so wonderful they should always *feel* wonderful. But in fact, *every* daughter goes through a period (which can last for years) where she feels inadequate and insecure.

What every teenage girl needs to realize is that every other girl feels the same way she does—they are all insecure and they are all constantly comparing themselves to each other. The girl with the beautiful long hair feels like a loser next to the girl who gets better grades. And the one with good grades wants to be like the girl who is great at dance. And the dancer feels badly about herself because she has fewer friends than the cheerleader. The more our girls understand that insecurity is a universal human trait, the better they will understand themselves and their peers.

What Do Good Friends Look Like?

I know some people assume that friendships between teenage girls are inevitably going to be complicated and painful, and often toxic. But in reality, many aren't. The trick lies in helping our daughters learn how to choose the right friends.

When older girls ask me for dating advice, I tell them to write down some non-negotiable character qualities they would want in a husband, such as integrity, patience, a good temperament, or a strong faith. If a boy doesn't meet the criteria, don't date him. Walking away a few days or weeks into a relationship is a whole lot easier than it is after months, or even years.

The same is true with girlfriends. If your daughter thinks of character qualities that she would want in a close friend, it can help her distinguish between superficial friendships and serious ones. I have found that this simple exercise gives girls confidence, helps them feel more in charge of their friendships, and provides understanding when those friendships don't work out.

Friends Share Common Interests, Beliefs, and Values

We celebrate diversity in our culture, and that can be a good thing. But it is also true that deep friendship relies on common bonds and interests. There is an enormous difference between close and casual friends. As adults, we know this because we have friends in each camp. With our daughters, they will naturally seek a few close friendships. We need to help them recognize that while they can be casual friends with many people—all it takes is kindness and politeness—close friendships are something to be nourished and cherished. Great friendships can be forged on a soccer field, in a classroom, in a church, or at a spelling bee, play, or concert—anything that brings girls together in a common activity that allows them to get to know one another so they can decide whether to open up and be more vulnerable. Most of all, deep friendships rely on shared core values. A girl who believes in being kind isn't going to be close with a girl who likes being mean. Another who values honesty and integrity won't want to be close to a friend who constantly lies. A girl interested in serving others and going on church-sponsored mission trips isn't likely to seek out a friend who is self-centered and focused on her appearance. A girl who doesn't want to be sexually active will have a harder time being friends with a girl who is sexually promiscuous.

Of course, girls can be acquaintances with girls who are very different, but having a deep, committed friendship is hard if they don't share common values. As parents, it is important for us to recognize what our girls believe and what their goals are in order to guide them into friendships that will be healthy. I have found that well-meaning parents often go in one of two directions in coaching their daughters on friendships.

Parents in one group want their daughters to befriend "the good kids," though the "good kids" are not necessarily defined by their characters. Some regard the "good kids" as the wealthiest or the most accomplished in sports or academics. It can be more about status than virtue.

Then there are parents who want their kids to be close friends with those who are less fortunate. While this can be a good thing, it can also lead to real trouble—not just because of the lack of parity in the relationship, but also because one of the girls might feel pressured to change, which can lead to resentment or bad behavior. This risk is greatly lessened if the girls share common values and interests and can inspire each other.

When Corinne and Amanda met, Corinne was living with foster parents. Corinne's parents were in jail, and she had been in foster care since she was six years old. Corinne had behaved well and was one of the lucky ones, staying with the same family instead of moving from home to home.

The two girls met in fifth grade. They were both smart and excelled at school, which made some of their classmates jealous. But feeling awkward, unathletic, and a little nerdy themselves, they formed a bond and became close friends.

During their years together, they talked about working with less fortunate kids. This seemed natural for Corinne because she had never felt loved by her biological parents and wanted to serve other kids who had been in similar situations. Amanda's parents, however, were devoted to her and she wanted other young girls to feel as well-loved as she had been.

In junior high school, they started babysitting. In high school, they expressed an interest in working at an orphanage. And over the course of a year, they raised enough money for a group service trip to Guatemala.

Along with two teachers and four other students, they spent a week caring for young children at a Guatemalan orphanage. They played with the children, fed them, and bathed them. They had a wonderful time and became so attached to the children that they wanted to adopt at least one of them. But the orphanage did not allow foreign adoptions, and they had to give up the idea.

Many may think of Amanda and Corinne as extraordinary young women, and in many ways they are. In other ways, however, they are very similar to other girls their age. I have found that when one girl lives with a deep desire to do something good, all it takes is another girl to fan the flames of that desire. Unfortunately for many of our girls, such dreams are squelched because we assume that such high-minded ideals are unrealistic, and sometimes we inadvertently *lead* our daughters into spending hours on social media and being self-centered because that's what we *expect*. Corinne and Amanda were encouraged by their parents, and some of their teachers and fellow students who admired their enthusiasm and what they set out to do joined them on the trip.

They Have Common Life Experiences

Girls who have gone through trauma, turmoil, depression, loss, deep grief, or other life-altering experiences often gravitate toward girls with similar backgrounds. These friendships can feel threatening to parents who feel that their daughter needs to get over the bad experience and who worry that the girls are sharing painful secrets that even the parents don't know. But in a way, that's the point—they can talk to these friends in a way that they can talk to no one else, knowing that they will understand and that they won't be upset by what is said. That's why girls need close girlfriends. They don't necessarily need advice; they need to know that they are not alone, that they don't have to live with shame, that they can be comforted, and that they can have hope for the future. Parents can try to do this for their daughters, and as parents we must stay involved. But sometimes it requires the close friendship of two girlfriends who have suffered in similar ways to provide that sort of healing. This need not be a threat to us as parents; in fact, if the friend is a good one, it can be a great help.

Helping Our Daughters Establish Healthy Relationships

The most crucial part of helping our daughters find, maintain, and develop healthy friendships is to stay closely connected to them. This means being invested in their lives, but not hovering over them. It's a balancing act that mothers in particular can find difficult, because in their effort to be always available to their daughters, they can look needy themselves—or they can intrude on a daughter's friendships in a way that's not constructive. All too often, mothers try to remain "close" to their daughters by joining them in their friendships, and girls don't like this. It is appropriate and helpful to become friendly with your daughter's friends—as long as you remember that you are a parent, not a peer. So don't friend your daughter's friends on Facebook. Your friends should be adults; hers should be her peers.

By maintaining an appropriate distance, you increase your authority—you are, after all, the adult. And you are in a great position to advise your daughter simply by listening—fully and with no hurry to respond so that she's invited to say more—and asking gentle questions that direct her to figure things out for herself. You know that girls, especially in middle school, can be very fickle in their friendships because they are immature and insecure. This can be completely normal, but it can also feel terrible if you're the girl being rejected—and the girls being rejected almost always blame themselves. This is where some careful parental questions can lead a girl to a better understanding that the problem might not be with her, but with her fickle friend. Many of your daughter's friendships take place on a far more superficial level than they think. Yes, rejection hurts. But with your help and encouragement, she will get over it and move forward; it's a simple part of growing up.

The fact that most girls are fickle doesn't mean you can't encourage your daughter to be a better friend. And parents can play a role in teaching their daughters what it means to be a kind, faithful friend. Though all children are self-centered, girls commit themselves to others relatively naturally—especially when encouraged by parents—and, as I have seen, their good behavior can be contagious among their peers.

In class one day when Lila was seventeen, she began shaking uncontrollably. Her eyes rolled back in her head and she fell to the ground. Classmates screamed. Her teachers recognized that she was having a seizure and called an ambulance. Within twenty-four hours, her life changed. She was diagnosed with a rare brain tumor. Her doctors told her that she would undergo months of radiation treatments, but that it might not be enough to save her life.

She was devastated. She was an outstanding student and had been looking forward to attending a stellar four-year college. Instead, she attended a local community college to be near the hospital that was treating her.

When the doctor's phone call came with Lila's diagnosis, her mother and Lila's friend Helen were with her. All three broke down sobbing.

When Lila began her radiation treatment, Helen would go to the hospital with her. She brought Lila gummy bears and ice cream—even when Lila was too nauseated from the radiation to eat them.

As Lila drew close to her twentieth birthday, both girls realized that the treatments weren't working. The tumor shrank but then grew again. During one of Lila's last hospitalizations, Helen contacted everyone she could think of to visit Lila and brighten her day. Scores of friends and acquaintances came to see her in the hospital. Lila told Helen, "Stop. I know what you're doing, and you don't need to. All I really want right now is you and my family. You are all enough."

Three days before Lila died, she was unable to speak or open her eyes. But she could squeeze Helen's hand. When she did, Helen opened a book of poetry that Lila loved and read from it. Hour after hour, she read to her friend.

On her last day, Lila's parents and sister sat with Helen at Lila's bedside. As they were chatting, Helen looked at Lila and realized that her best friend was gone. It took nine months before she could think of Lila without crying. Eventually, Helen moved forward with her life and finished college. Lila's courage and academic prowess remained an inspiration. Our daughters need such good and loyal friends. As parents, we can help them recognize and pursue true friendship—the sort of friendships that can transform their lives forever.

Chapter Eleven

Help Her Be a Strong Woman, Not a Victim

M ore than twenty-five years ago, author Charles J. Sykes wrote a book called *A Nation of Victims: The Decay of the American Character*, which is about how it had become popular to declare oneself and even define oneself as a victim.[1] Another word for that is self-pity, and the problem he identified has gotten far worse since then.

Self-pity is toxic because it paralyzes people and prevents them from taking responsibility for their own actions and helping themselves. It blames others for failures and makes personal success seem impossible. We need our daughters to be strong, not self-pitying.

Elena came to me for her second-grade school physical. She was eight and was having trouble getting along with her peers. She told me she didn't like going to school because her classmates made fun of her and no one there liked her. Her mother chimed in and agreed, saying that Elena was an outcast at school because she was fat and had red hair. "Poor thing—life is hard for a girl like Elena who feels different."

I reviewed Elena's growth chart. She was terribly overweight—by forty pounds. She sat on my exam table hunched forward with her hands crossed in front of her belly. Her mother said, "We've talked about cutting back calories, but, well, I don't want her self-esteem to suffer."

Elena's mother spoke in a soothing and soft voice, but Elena was hostile and interrupted her mother several times, saying that she was embarrassing her and needed to zip it. It was clear who drove the bus at home. It wasn't Elena's mother.

When I finished the exam, I addressed her weight issues gingerly in a way that I hoped would make mother and daughter listen. I said, "Many girls in elementary school are too focused on weight and appearance, which isn't healthy. But that isn't Elena's problem. She's having a hard time getting control of her intake, and that concerns me because the weight she's adding on puts her at risk for diabetes and other problems that could follow her into adulthood."

Her mother said, "I know what you say is true, in general, Dr. Meeker, but you don't understand—Elena really doesn't eat that much."

"Alright, let's review her diet. Elena, what do you eat for breakfast?"

Her mother jumped in and answered for her. "She likes French toast and Cocoa Puffs—usually a little of each, not much though. Then she gets dressed for school and has a snack. I always let her have a snack because I don't want her to have low blood sugar in the morning when she's trying to concentrate at school."

"Mom, you are so exaggerating. I never eat that much."

Her mother shook her head.

"And what about lunch?" I asked. "Do you eat the school lunch, or do you pack your own?"

"I usually eat the school lunch because we're too busy to make lunch. My mom could make it the night before, but she won't. Other kids' moms do, but she doesn't."

Her mother ignored the criticism and said, "Oh, Elena, you forgot to tell her that you have a snack before lunch. Remember, you take a bagel with cream cheese. But really, Dr. Meeker, she never finishes it."

"Okay, what about the rest of the day?"

"Well, at school, I usually have chicken nuggets, chocolate milk, and juice. I have a snack when I come home, then I play outside a lot. For dinner, my mom usually calls in a pizza, or warms up a frozen pizza, or makes pasta. But I never eat much for dinner."

"That's true," said her mother. "I don't understand how she could be gaining weight."

"Well," I said, "I think I can see the problem, and I can help if you'll agree to make some small changes. First, let's cut out the extra food at breakfast. Can you do that?"

Elena scowled at me. "No! I am so hungry in the morning. I can't do that."

Her mother agreed. "That would be hard—and I don't think it's a good idea. She needs to concentrate at school; she needs those calories."

"Okay, what about skipping her morning snack, then?"

"She can try, but I don't think that's going to work. She packs her bagel herself and needs it to get through the morning."

It soon became clear that neither mother nor daughter was willing to change, so I tried a different tack with her mother. "Dinner is entirely within your control. I need you to cook healthy meals at night and limit Elena to one plate, one serving. Elena, do you like chicken, vegetables, or salad?"

Elena glared at her mother and shouted, "NO!"

"She won't eat anything but pasta or pizza, Dr. Meeker. I wish she would try other foods, but she won't."

"She needs to change her diet for the sake of her health."

"It's not that bad, doctor. She's already struggling with being overweight. I don't want to put any extra burden on her. With the kids making fun of her at school, I want her to be comfortable at home."

"Unless you and your daughter are willing to make changes, Elena's health will suffer. She could easily become a diabetic. She has the beginnings of a serious problem. We can correct it now, but it will take effort. You and she have got to be willing to make that effort."

"Dr. Meeker, I understand your concern, but she's young and vulnerable and sensitive about the kids at school making fun of her. I think focusing on her diet right now would be a mistake. I think we need to focus on her self-esteem instead."

They left the examination room, and my heart sank. Elena was trapped because her mother felt sorry for her. She felt she couldn't or didn't need to change. She was a *victim* of obesity, and that was unfair. Other kids didn't have to struggle the way she did.

As much as I'd like to say that this attitude is rare, it isn't. Many parents see their children as perpetual victims of unfairness. I see parents yell at coaches because their daughter isn't getting enough playing time. They complain about teachers who give their daughters poor grades. They complain about employers who demand punctuality at work and politeness to customers—even when their daughters don't feel like turning up or being polite. Too often, parents teach their daughters that the bumps and bruises they encounter in life are always someone else's fault. They do so with the best of intentions—they don't want their daughters to feel terrible—but with the worst of results. They actually make things miserable for their daughters. Constantly blaming others does not make anyone happy. Denying our daughters' personal responsibility means denying them the means to improve themselves and to be truly happy and successful.

If Elena's mother had simply told her, "Changing your diet is going to be hard, but you can do it and I will help," she would have taken her daughter from self-pitying powerlessness (and the bad attitude that comes with it) to strength. Elena not only needed to lose weight, but she needed her mother to teach her that life is about choices. She could choose to lie down and feel sorry for herself, or she could hit the problem head on and win.

The sad truth is that Elena will probably remain obese for years, and her mother's efforts to maintain Elena's self-esteem will actually undermine it. Elena's failure to get her weight under control will inevitably lead to poor self-esteem, physical limitations, and resentment of others—and all because she was treated like a weak girl instead of a strong one.

Parents are in a tough spot. We want our kids to be happy and have good self-esteem, but the trick is that happiness and self-esteem are actually products of taking personal responsibility, working hard, keeping faith and hope, and developing personal mastery and independence. But rather than push kids to act independently, we too often do things for them or we excuse them when they make mistakes for which they should take full responsibility. I have done this, and I expect you have too.

We default to blaming others because we don't want to believe that our kids would do something wrong and we don't want to think we have failed as parents. The fact is that usually when kids make a mistake, it's not because they're bad or because they have bad parents, *but it's because they are kids.*

We're also prone to blame others because it's a way to avoid conflict. If we recognize that our daughter did something bad, we would have to deal with it and show her the consequences. Many parents have difficulty with confrontation, discipline, and setting rules. In my experience, many parents will start off strong before giving in. They will, for instance, confiscate their daughter's phone for a week as punishment, but then cut deals when their daughter pushes back and complains about them being mean or unfair.

Parents have a balancing act to perform. We are the most important people in our children's lives, and yet we cannot let our children become the center of our lives. We need distance to judge them objectively and be good parents to them, and they need distance to develop independence. Putting our children at the center of our lives warps the dynamics of a healthy family. Parents should be in charge. We should not jump at our children's every wish. In truth, they don't want that kind of power; they want their parents to be leaders, to provide structure and guidelines and enforce the rules. When we act otherwise, we merely make them selfish, and selfish people aren't happy people; they blame others for their own failings.

Of course, parents often don't recognize when this dynamic is happening in their home. They might sense something is wrong, they might feel tension, they mind find themselves resentful of their children, but they can't put their fingers on why. To diffuse the tension, or out of guilt for their feelings of resentment, parents might become overly permissive, which only makes things worse. Arguments ensue, daughters storm out of the house, and parents feel they have lost control. And they have.

What Are the Ramifications for Daughters?

When daughters receive the wrong kind of attention and are doted upon, they have a false sense of self and the world around them. They become so used to people elevating their every want, need, or desire that they become resentful of those around them who don't "appreciate" them. This happened to Calista.

When Calista was thirteen, her gymnastics coach pulled her parents aside and told them that she had unusual talent—even Olympic-level talent—if she continued to develop her skills at her current rate. Calista's parents were elated. A year later, they asked her coach what they should do to maximize her potential. Calista's coach was cautious, saying that Calista's progress had slowed down.

Her parents had difficulty hearing this. Her father said, "We're thinking about moving to California. We know Calista is extraordinary for her age, and we've found a gymnastics training center there that looks exceptional."

Her coach said, "I don't think she's ready for a gymnastic center. The kids who go there have training at the forefront of their life—everything else, including school, is organized around it. It's rigorous, and Calista needs to mature in her athletic skills before you even think about a big move like that."

Her father said, "We've thought about it, and we're committed to doing it. We want to give her every opportunity to go to the Olympics."

"What about your two younger children?" asked the coach. "It's a sacrifice for them too."

"They're on board," said Calista's mother. "We all think it's so exciting."

The coach made one last plea. "I honestly think that this is premature. Yes, Calista is talented, but there are thousands of girls who are more talented. She will be working among some of the most competitive, successful gymnasts in the world. She's a very good gymnast, but I don't think she's ready for that."

Calista's parents went home discouraged and reconsidered their plans. Over the ensuing months, as they watched Calista practice, they again convinced themselves that she had Olympic-level talent. They sold their home, packed up their three kids, and moved to California.

The following three years went smoothly for Calista, but not for her eight-year-old brother. He had difficulty making friends at his new school. His mother frequently consoled him, saying, "I know it's hard, honey, but don't you want Calista to go to the Olympics? Wouldn't it be fun to travel far away and see other countries?"

Calista's brother was assuaged for a while, but it didn't last; school never got better for him. Calista worked very hard at gymnastics and she did well at her first national gymnastics competition. But then at the Junior Olympics, she performed poorly and said she wasn't feeling well. When Olympic tryouts finally rolled around, she didn't make the cut. She came home and cried to her parents.

"I can't believe this," she said. "I know I was better than some of those girls. Besides, I worked harder than they did. I think that the judges were biased. One of the judges barely watched my routines. It just isn't fair."

"I know," said her father. "Sometimes judges aren't fair. They may be having a bad day. But to miss you and think that you aren't better than many of those girls shows you how biased some of them can be. You're taller than many of the girls. I'll bet they didn't like that. I'll see what I can do. You at least deserve another tryout."

Calista's father called her coach and told her that the tryouts were unfair. Couldn't the judges see how good she was? By some miracle, he talked the committee into letting her try out one more time. But again, she wasn't put on the team.

Calista's parents felt devastated. They had disrupted the lives of everyone in their family only to see their daughter's Olympic dreams denied. They stayed in California for four more years to give her another shot at the Olympics. But again, "biased" judges didn't appreciate her talent.

So the family packed up again and returned to Michigan. Calista's siblings were thrilled to be reunited with their old friends and were happy at school.

Calista applied to six prestigious colleges in New England. To her surprise, she was rejected by each one. She complained again that they didn't know how talented she really was. She also applied for several jobs working with young gymnasts. That brought her a job offer, but when they told her that the pay was thirty-five thousand dollars per year and that sometimes she'd have work more than forty hours a week, she exclaimed, "Are you kidding me? Have you read my resume? I moved to California to work with one of the finest trainers in the United States. I tried out for the Olympics twice and was only cut because of biased judges. I won't take anything less than ninety-five thousand dollars a year."

Needless to say, she didn't get that job or any of the other coaching jobs she applied for. She felt that the world was against her, and her parents agreed. Eventually, she found a career in retail sales, but she remained resentful that she never got the recognition that she felt was her due.

Most parents don't take their daughters' wishes to such an extreme, but less dramatic variations of this scenario happen in homes across America all the time. Many parents rearrange their schedules in order to accommodate opportunities for their daughters. Without even realizing it, these commitments can become the central family dynamic. Siblings put up with one parent leaving each weekend to attend a daughter's competitive events. Parents talk about the success of their daughter, and she comes to believe that her success is important not only to her, but to her entire family. Then she feels pressure to keep performing. She sees her family sacrifice time and money for her. Family meals are passed over so that she can practice. Over the years, she comes to believe that it is not only good that her parents accommodate her, but that it is her right.

But then life happens. When high school is over, she gives up her sport because she has lost interest, or isn't good enough to play in college, or needs to focus more on her studies, or because she has entered the workforce and doesn't have time for it. Suddenly, her identity seems rearranged. No one focuses on her achievements anymore; away from home, she's no longer the center of anyone's world. In many ways until this time, her parents and siblings served her. And now she begins to learn a painful lesson: she has to take responsibility for her life. Unfortunately, she feels cheated; she had assumed that having things done for her was a healthy and normal part of her existence. That will make her transition to maturity much more painful than it needs to be.

This isn't a parent blame game. Many of the mistakes we make as parents we make because we love our daughters. But we also do make mistakes because we do what our friends do. Our daughters have peer pressure, and so do we. When we see our friends jump to their daughters' needs, we follow suit. But this is not the way to develop strong, hardworking, independent, and creative women. Instead—and this is ironic in an age of feminism—we are teaching our daughters that they need *others* to make things happen for *them*.

Changing Perspective

The important thing is to raise daughters who realize that they are *not* the center of the family, but are part of a whole. One easy way to do this is to have your daughter do family chores. However much she might complain about it, it actually makes her feel needed, which makes her feel good. Often, in fact, it's not that daughters balk at helping around the house; it is that their parents don't want their daughters giving up precious time when they could be practicing the piano or pursuing their other talents. It is perfectly normal for parents to be proud of their daughters, but we need to take pride in their formation and development as mature human beings who remember that they are first and foremost part of a family, that they have obligations that extend beyond themselves, and that they are personally responsible for their own successes and failures.

Train for Independence, Not Dependence

Parents love to be needed. Mothers, in particular, feel that meeting their children's needs makes them a better parent. But doting on children does nothing to make them successful and happy adults. Many parents have a hard time realizing that as our children develop, what they need from mom and dad develops as well, and part of that is preparing them to be independent.

My sister-in-law suffered from breast cancer in her forties and uterine cancer in her fifties. Sadly, cancer took her life as she neared the young age of sixty. What made her death more tragic was that she was a single mother of four grown children ranging in age from nineteen to twenty-seven; the youngest was in her first year of college.

As she lay dying, she told my husband, "I have lived a wonderful life. I'm not worried about my kids because they don't need me anymore."

At first her comment upset me. *Of course, they do!* I thought. *You are their only parent, what will they do now?* Then I realized the truth in what she was saying—but as a mother, I didn't want to believe it. Her kids *didn't* need her. She had raised them to be strong and independent. While she felt very close to each one of them, and they to her, she had taught them through her divorce and two bouts of cancer that they could live well on their own. They could manage finances, make good decisions about choosing a spouse, hold good jobs, and work hard. She had full confidence that they would be good parents to her future grandchildren. She had taught them everything they needed to stand on their own.

Many parents have a hard time shifting gears as their children grow up because their own identities have become almost entirely that of a mother or father. These roles have given them great fulfillment and joy and they don't want to lose that; they believe their happiness is dependent upon being needed by their daughters. Such parents want to keep making decisions for their daughters. Some daughters will rebel against this, which creates conflict. But if a daughter accepts it, it creates dependence. The daughter might call four times a week, visit frequently, and even ask her mother to do her laundry and change her sheets because, after all, she couldn't possibly have the time as a busy, young career woman.

Families are there to help one another—but not so that parents end up doing what their children can do for themselves. When we do that, we inadvertently teach them that they are incapable. For a daughter, this can lead to a great deal of personal insecurity.

One patient of mine named Emma didn't go to college; she went to work. But she did not become independent. Her parents let her live with them and paid her bills so she could save money. They didn't ask her to cook or clean or help with chores because they wanted her to focus on doing well at her job.

But after a few years, sparks began to fly. Emma's parents were appalled that she kept changing jobs, was not advancing in a career, and was actually going into reverse, moving from full-time work to part-time work. Her bosses were never nice. She couldn't get along with her coworkers because they were unfair. She thought her parents needed to be more understanding. But they were tired of paying her bills and waiting for her to live on her own. They needed to save for their retirement, and her "needs" were getting in the way.

When they told Emma that she had to move out, she exploded. They were cruel and unfair, she yelled. They didn't care about her because if they did, she insisted, they would never tell her to leave. She refused to go, her parents gave in, and all three continue to live unhappily together.

With the best of intentions, her parents created a monster by giving Emma one loud, clear message: you need us to survive; you can't be independent because you aren't strong enough. In the end, they weren't strong enough to undo that devastatingly harmful message.

How to Keep Her Strong

There are a few key steps every parent can take to ensure that their daughter becomes as strong as she possibly can be.

Give Her Opportunities to Work Hard Alone

Any parent can start this with a young child. Recently, my two-year-old granddaughter was putting on her jacket. I let her try alone, but she wasn't getting her arms in the right sleeves. After a few minutes, I grabbed the jacket and put it on her correctly because I was in a hurry to get somewhere. But after I zipped the coat up, she screamed. Then she cried. She wanted to put her coat on and be successful, and I took that away from her. I would like to say that I pulled her jacket off and gave her another try, but I didn't. In the moment, I was frustrated and needed her to get in the car. But the next time, I changed course. When we were ready to go outside a week later, the same scenario came up. I gave her the jacket, and again she kept putting it on backwards. I turned it the right way and gave it back. She put the jacket on backwards over and over again, and I was getting frustrated. But I realized that even at age two she needed to understand struggle and capability. If I took her struggle away, she would have never won her personal battle.

This was a small incident, but if you are impatient like I am, it seems to last forever. We need to remember, though, that victories that seem small and insignificant to us are enormous for our children and grandchildren. After what seemed liked her thirtieth attempt, she finally put her jacket on the right way and beamed. There were no tears or screams because she experienced the joy of success. And even overcoming that small obstacle started a foundation for her to build more and larger successes on top of it.

Show Her How to Live Fearlessly

Our natural instinct as parents is to protect our daughters. Fathers, in particular, feel protective—and this is good and healthy.

But it is possible to protect our daughters too much. Without realizing it, we can coddle them and prevent them from learning how to face fear and defend themselves. As adults, we've learned to press on while suffering from anxiety, fatigue, or stress. Our kids need to learn that too. We worry that something bad might happen—and it might—but we cannot control every circumstance in their lives. They have to learn to work through tough situations. We can help teach them by showing courage ourselves.

Kristine was awakened by her four-year-old daughter Jenna, who had developed a horrible-sounding cough in the middle of the night. Because they were on a Christmas visit to Kristine's family's home in rural Montana, Jenna's pediatrician was unavailable. So Kristine decided to take her to the local hospital emergency room.

The emergency room physician examined Jenna and told Kristine he was ordering a chest X-ray to ensure that she didn't have pneumonia. He also told her that he was ordering some blood work. About an hour later, he came back. His face was ashen. "I'm not exactly sure what is going on with your daughter," he said, "but we need to get her to Seattle Children's Hospital right away. She doesn't have pneumonia. In fact, I'm concerned that she has some type of cancer—perhaps leukemia."

He left the room and ordered an ambulance to take Kristine and Jenna on the five-hour trek to Seattle. The roads were icy, but that was the last thing on Kristine's mind. She boarded the back of the ambulance with her daughter hooked up to an IV and their journey began. Little did she know that it was the beginning of three years of pain.

To complicate matters, Kristine left her two-year-old daughter behind with her parents. She worried about her. And her husband was halfway across the world serving in the military. How desperately she wanted him with her. All alone with her daughter struggling to breathe, Kristine sat and waited.

During the arduous ambulance ride, I spoke with Kristine on the phone. Her voice was surprisingly calm, but I knew she was already thinking of the worst-case scenario: her beautiful daughter's death.

Kristine talked me through everything that had happened during the previous eight hours. Jenna was fine. She ate a good dinner. She didn't have a fever. As she put her to bed, she noticed that Jenna seemed anxious, and she had never seen her anxious before. But after Kristine left the room, Jenna fell sound asleep until her cough woke her up. At first, she told me, she thought she had the flu. But soon she knew that something more was going on. "Maybe I should have brought her to the ER sooner. Maybe I should have noticed her paleness. Or maybe...."

I tried to stop her. Maybes were irrelevant and wouldn't have made a bit of difference. Sometimes for reasons we will never understand, kids just get sick. They, like adults, can be stricken with a life-threatening illness in a matter of moments.

As worried as she had to be, Kristina then said something I will never forget: "I have a tremendous peace. Here I am alone in the middle of nowhere with my daughter who has who-knows-what, and I believe that God has everything under control. I can't do anything. But He can. I don't know how this will all end. But God's got this. And He is good."

When she said this, I felt overwhelmed. And in a way, I felt very weak. The faith of this young mother sitting beside her daughter who was fighting for her life was extraordinary. Her words weren't rehearsed platitudes. They were real. They spilled from a broken heart.

Kristine's words reminded me of a scene from C. S. Lewis's *The Voyage of the Dawn Treader.*

"But no one except Lucy knew that as it circled the mast it had whispered to her, 'Courage, dear heart,' and the voice, she felt sure, was Aslan's, and with the voice a delicious smell breathed in her face."[2]

Jenna was diagnosed with acute lymphocytic leukemia and was immediately placed in the intensive care unit. She had a tumor in her chest that was so large that it was pushing against her airway. Her situation was dire. If they couldn't get the tumor to shrink immediately, her airway could be closed off and she would die.

Kristine's husband was flown to the hospital and Jenna began treatment for her leukemia. After six weeks, she returned to Michigan and began a long road of chemotherapy, blood tests, spinal taps, X-rays, and tests too numerous to count. She lost her hair, was swollen from steroids,

and suffered nausea from the chemotherapy. About a year into her treatment, I met with Kristine and Jenna. Her mother said that the young girl
was enduring her therapy very well. I asked Jenna what she thought of
going to the hospital (two hours away from their home) so often and
getting tests. "Oh, I dunno," she said. "They're not all that bad. The
nurses are really nice. But I don't like those pokes in my back."

I was struck by Jenna and Kristine's matter-of-fact attitudes. Leukemia was just something she had to deal with and that needed treatment.
There was no sense of self-pity. Life went on and Kristina treated her
daughter the same as before—including scolding her when she misbe-
haved. Leukemia would be no excuse for bad behavior.

Many parents who have had a child with a chronic (but not life-
threatening) illness like asthma or anemia tell me to handle their child
gently. If the child screams the moment that I touch her, the parent grabs
the child out of pity, saying, "She just doesn't like doctors. She's been
traumatized so much by needles." Then they proceed to coo and swoon
over their child.

Unlike Kristine, they have not taught their child courage—the need
to be strong in the face of fear, to be tough because pain is part of life.
This excerpt from the poem "Courage" by Robert W. Service sums up
Kristine's attitude:

> Today I opened wide my eyes,
> And stared with wonder and surprise,
> To see beneath November skies
> An apple blossom peer;
> Upon a branch as bleak as night
> It gleamed exultant on my sight,
> A fairy beacon burning bright
> Of hope and cheer.
> "Alas!" said I, "poor foolish thing,
> Have you mistaken this for Spring?
> Behold, the thrush has taken wing,

And Winter's near."
Serene it seemed to lift its head:
"The Winter's wrath I do not dread,
Because I am," it proudly said,
"A Pioneer.
"Some apple blossom must be first,
With beauty's urgency to burst
Into a world for joy athirst,
And so I dare;
And I shall see what none shall see -
December skies gloom over me,
And mock them with my April glee,
And fearless fare."

Courage isn't about having no fear. It is about pushing through the fear and doing what is best—for ourselves and our kids. How easy it is to feel sorry for our daughters because of a toxic culture that leads them astray, or because they suffer from anxiety, depression, or a chronic illness, or because they had to endure a horrible divorce between their parents.

But we do them a tremendous disservice if we teach them to blame the world for their problems, because if others are to blame, then they are helpless and stuck. But girls who have been taught to find and develop their inner strength will always have hope and live more fully.

Help Her Take Reasonable Risks and Fail

It would be irresponsible, of course, for any parent to encourage his or her daughter to take a risk that would have life-altering consequences. Many parents make this mistake, particularly with teenagers. Believing they are more mature than they really are, some parents give far too much freedom to their teen daughters because, as they say, they can "trust" them. They may ask for birth control for their sixteen-year-old because she has a "nice" boyfriend, they know she will be sexually active, and they don't want any problems. In their naiveté they fail to realize that pregnancy isn't the only "problem"—birth control won't protect her from depression and many sexually transmitted diseases.

Other parents allow their daughter to go to a weekend party at a friend's house where they think drinking might be going on. The parents who own the home might not be there, but since their daughter is a straight-A student, she can go and be trusted not to do something stupid (or against the law). But no matter how good she is, her brain isn't fully mature, and teens—particularly in groups—can't always be trusted to do the right thing *because they are kids.*

That being said, our daughters do need to learn how to step out of their comfort zones and take *appropriate* risks. Most girls won't do this on their own because they want to be successful, which means sticking to what they know. But no girl will succeed in life if she doesn't learn to fail well, and that means learning that you don't have to be good at everything to be a good person.

When Anna was in tenth grade, she showed that she could excel in math and history. Academics came relatively easy to her and she didn't feel challenged. She liked field hockey but always felt that she wasn't a good athlete, so she never tried out for a team. She considered playing in the marching band, but again doubted that her drum skills were good enough to make it. Her parents, enjoying her academic success, didn't want to see Anna struggle, so they never pushed her to try something new. So Anna stayed comfortable and watched her friends play field hockey and play in the marching band.

When she went away to college, she continued to excel at academics but became bored. She collected her courage and tried out for a women's choir group. During her audition, she noticed some students in the audience snickering.

"Thank you, Anna," the choir director said. "We'll get back to you. But I need to tell you that singing may not be one of your strengths."

Anna was embarrassed. A couple of days later, the choir director called her and said they didn't have a slot for her. She was upset but not surprised. What did surprise her was how quickly she got over the rejection. In fact, she told me that in some strange way the rejection gave her the courage to try other things. "I decided, what do I have to lose? The worst that can happen is that they tell me no—and that's not so bad."

She tried out for club field hockey twice—and failed to make the team both times. "Yeah, I felt bad about that," she conceded, "but I didn't feel like a bad person. When the choir rejected me, I felt very ashamed, like I was a real loser. But with the field hockey team, I tried my best, and yeah, I felt bad for a few days, but I moved on."

The wonderful thing for Anna was that the more she was rejected, the more she resolved to get into an extracurricular activity on campus. "After a while," she told me, "it kind of became like a game. In a weird way, it was fun; it was sort of a way to test myself outside of the classroom. I tried out for marching band and didn't get in. I tried out for club swimming and failed at that. But then I tried out for our college band. They needed a drummer, and there I was. I made it. I enjoyed it. And I did it every year."

As parents, we don't want our daughters to experience failure. We are afraid that their self-esteem will suffer. But it is through experiencing failure and overcoming it that our daughters learn resilience and that failure in one thing—or in several things—doesn't mean their life is over. Failing is an inevitable part of life—and part of growing up is learning and growing stronger from it.

So the next time your awkward daughter wants to try out for ice hockey, encourage her to do it. If your third-grade daughter has never shown an aptitude for science but wants to compete in a science fair, let her. And if your daughter is only an average speller but wants to enter a spelling competition, tell her she'll have to study hard for it, but let her push herself and give it a go.

After you have encouraged your daughter to reach beyond her comfort zone and maybe fall down, you can show her that you value her regardless of whether she is good or bad at something, or whether she wins or loses. You can teach her that falling down isn't as painful as it seems. You can teach her to push through her fears. These are all liberating lessons.

Never Do for Her What She Can Do for Herself

We all want to help our daughters, but we must keep this desire in check. I have done many things for my daughters that I shouldn't have done. But we all do; almost every parent is guilty of this. We sweep behind our daughters and finish tasks they were supposed to do. Ellie forgot to feed the dog, so we do it. Vera hasn't made her bed for a week, so we do it because we can't stand looking at a mess. Nora is supposed to clean up after dinner, but she says she has too much homework. So we clean the kitchen. Jana can tie her shoes, but since she's always late for school, we tie them for her.

These are small things, but they set an unhealthy pattern for our daughters. They learn that if they don't do something, they don't have to worry. We will do it for them. This can become a very bad habit as they grow older. So begin early in making your daughter accountable for the actions you request. If you ask her to do something, make sure that she does the work. Teach her that she can accomplish things, that she can manage the time to do both her chores and her schoolwork, that she can be personally responsible, and that she has a commitment to help others in the family.

Give your daughter the gift that will serve her well for life: teach her to be strong in character, will, and resolve and to never feel pity for herself.

Acknowledgments

I want to thank Marji Ross for her constant support and encouragement, as well as my fabulous editors, Harry Crocker and Kathryn Riggs, for making the book much better than I could. I want to express my gratitude to my patients for giving me the privilege of caring for them over the last thirty years. To Anne Mann and Lisbeth Keen—I am so grateful for the ways you have kept me on track and organized my life. To Shane Koefed and Ameera Masud, thank you for the hundreds of hours you have put into my work. You are both amazing.

And to my wonderful husband, Walt—you have hung in there with me for three decades, and for that I am enormously grateful. Finally, to my amazing daughters and granddaughters—I am so proud that you are and will be strong women.

Bibliography

"Family Guide to Prime Time Television." Parents Television Council, http://w2.parentstv.org/main/Toolkit/FamilyGuide.aspx.

"Media Violence: An Examination of Violence, Graphic Violence, and Gun Violence in the Media." Parents Television Council, December 2013, http://w2.parentstv.org/main/Research/Studies/CableViolence/vstudy_dec2013.pdf.

Abdel-Khalek, Ahmed M. "Can Somatic Symptoms Predict Depression?" *Social Behavior and Personality: An International Journal* 32, no. 7 (2004): 657–66.

Adams, Paul L., Judith R. Milner and Nancy A. Schrepf. *Fatherless Children*. New York: John Wiley, 1984.

Akerlof, George A., Janet L. Yellen, and Michael L. Katz. "An Analysis of Out-of-Wedlock Childbearing in the United States." *Quarterly Journal of Economics* 111, no. 2 (May 1996): 277–317.

Allen, J. P., F. C. McFarland, M. R. Porter, and P. Marsh. "The Two Faces of Adolescents' Success with Peers: Adolescent Popularity, Social Adaptation, and Deviant Behavior." *Child Development* 76, no. 3 (2005): 747–60.

Allen, Sarah, and Kerry Daly. "The Effects of Father Involvement: A Summary of the Research Evidence." Father Involvement Initiative—Ontario Network 1 (Fall 2002), http://www.ecdip.org/docs/pdf/IF%20Father%20Res%20Summary%20(KD).pdf.

American Academy of Child & Adolescent Psychiatry. "Suicide in Children and Teens." June 2018, https://www.aacap.org/AACAP/Families_and_Youth/Facts_for_Families/FFF-Guide/Teen-Suicide-010.aspx.

Anderson, S. E., and Aviva Must. "Interpreting the Continued Decline in Average Age at Menarche: Results from Two Nationally Representative Surveys of U.S. Girls Studied 10 Years Apart." *Journal of Pediatrics* 147, no. 6 (December 2005): 753–60.

Anderson, S. E., G. E. Dallal, and Aviva Must. "Relative Weight and Race Influence Average Age at Menarche: Results from Two Nationally Representative Surveys of US Girls Studied 25 Years Apart." *Pediatrics* 111, no. 4 (April 2003): 844–50.

Andrade L., J. J. Caraveo-Anduago, P. Berglund, R. V. Bijl, R. De Graaf, W. Vollebergh, E. Dragomirecka, R. Kohn, M. Keller, R. C. Kessler, N. Kawakami, C. Kilic, D. Offord, T. B. Ustun, and H. U. Wittchen. "Epidemiology of Major Depressive Episodes: Results from the International Consortium of Psychiatric Epidemiology (ICPE) Surveys." *International Journal of Methods in Psychiatric Research* 12, no. 1 (2003): 3–21.

Armsden, Gay C., and Mark T. Greenberg. "Inventory of Parent and Peer Attachment: Revised Manual." (Unpublished revised version) Seattle: University of Washington, 1989.

____. "The Inventory of Parent and Peer Attachment: Individual Differences and Their Relationship to Psychological Well-Being in Adolescence." *Journal of Youth and Adolescence* 16, no. 5 (October 1987): 427–54.

Atzil, Shir, Talma Hendler, Oma Zagoory-Sharon, Yonatan Winetraub, and Ruth Feldman. "Synchrony and Specificity in the Maternal and the Paternal Brain: Relations to Oxytocin and Vasopressin." *Journal of the American Academy of Child & Adolescent Psychiatry* 51, no. 8 (August 2012): 798–811.

Bem, Sandra L. *The Lenses of Gender: Transforming the Debate on Sexual Inequality.* New Haven, Connecticut: Yale University Press, 1993.

Berndt, T. J., and R. C. Savin-Williams. "Variations in Friendships and Peer-group Relationships in Adolescence." In *Handbook of Clinical Research and Practice with Adolescents*, edited by P. Tolan and B. Cohler, 203–19. New York: John Wiley, 1993.

Bilenberg, N., D. J. Petersen, K. Hoerder, and C. Gillberg. "The Prevalence of Child-Psychiatric Disorders among 8–9-Year-Old Children in Danish Mainstream Schools." *Acta Psychiatrica Scandinavica* 111, no. 1 (January 2005): 59–67.

Biller, Henry B. "Paternal and Sex-Role Factors in Cognitive and Academic Functioning." *Nebraska Symposium on Motivation* 21, 83–123.

Bitsko R. H., J. R. Holbrook, R. M. Ghandour, S. J. Blumberg, S. N. Visser, R. Perou, and J. Walkup. "Epidemiology and Impact of Healthcare Provider–Diagnosed Anxiety and Depression among US Children." *Journal of Developmental and Behavioral Pediatrics* 39, no. 5 (June 2018): 395–403.

Bjørnskov, Christian, Axel Dreher, and Justina A. V. Fischer. "On Gender Inequality and Life Satisfaction: Does Discrimination Matter?" Economics Discussion Paper No. 2007-07, University of St. Gallen, April 23, 2007.

Bogaert, Anthony F. "Menarche and Father Absence in a National Probability Sample." *Journal of Biosocial Science* 40, no. 4 (2008): 623–36.

Bronstein, Phyllis. "Father-Child Interaction: Implications for Gender-Role Socialization." In *Fatherhood Today: Men's Changing Role in the Family*, edited by P. Bronstein and C. P. Cowan, 107–24. Oxford, England: John Wiley, 1988.

Brown, G. W., B. Andrews, T. Harris, Z. Adler, and L. Bridge. "Social Support, Self-Esteem and Depression." *Psychological Medicine* 16, no. 4 (November 1986): 813–31.

Buhrmester, D. "Intimacy of Friendship, Interpersonal Competence, and Adjustment during Preadolescence and Adolescence." *Child Development* 61, no. 4 (August 1990): 1101–11.

Bukowski, W. M., C. Gauze, B. Hoza, and A. F. Newcomb. "Differences and Consistency Between Same-Sex and Other-Sex Peer Relations during Early Adolescence." *Developmental Psychology* 29, no. 2 (1993): 255–64.

Centers for Disease Control and Prevention. "Data and Statistics on Children's Mental Health." https://www.cdc.gov/childrensmentalhealth/data.html.

____. "National Health and Nutrition Examination Survey." National Center for Health Statistics, https://www.cdc.gov/nchs/nhanes/index.htm?CDC_AA_refVal=https%3A%2F%2Fwww.cdc.gov%2Fnchs%2Fnhanes.htm.

____. "National Survey of the Diagnosis and Treatment of ADHD and Tourette Syndrome." National Center for Health Statistics, https://www.cdc.gov/nchs/slaits/ns_data.htm.

____. "National Youth Tobacco Survey (NYTS)." Smoking & Tobacco Use, https://www.cdc.gov/tobacco/data_statistics/surveys/nyts/index.htm.

____. "School Health Policies and Practices Study (SHPPS)." Adolescent and School Health, https://www.cdc.gov/healthyyouth/data/shpps/index.htm.

____. "School-Associated Violent Death Study." Violence Prevention, https://www.cdc.gov/violenceprevention/youthviolence/schoolviolence/savd.html.

Chisholm, J. S., J. A. Quinlivan, R. W. Petersen, and D. A. Coall. "Early Stress Predicts Age at Menarche and First Birth, Adult Attachment, and Expected Lifespan." *Human Nature* 16, no. 3 (2005): 233–65.

Cohen, P., J. Cohen, S. Kasen, C. N. Velez, C. Hartmark, J. Johnson, M. Rojas, and E. L. Streuning. "An Epidemiological Study of Disorders in Late Childhood and Adolescence--I. Age- and Gender-Specific Prevalence." *Journal of Child Psychology and Psychiatry* 34, no. 6 (September 1993): 851–67.

Coker, A. L., K. E. Davis, I. Arias, S. Desai, M. Sanderson, H. M. Brandt, P. H. Smith. "Physical and Mental Health Effects of Intimate Partner Violence for Men and Women." *American Journal of Preventative Medicine* 23, no. 4 (November 2002): 260–8.

Costello, E. J., S. Mustillo, A. Erkanli, G. Keeler, and A. Angold. "Prevalence and Development of Psychiatric Disorders in Childhood and Adolescence." *Archives of General Psychiatry* 60, no. 8 (August 2003): 837–44.

Cree, R. A., R. H. Bitsko, L. R. Robinson, J. R. Holbrook, M. L. Danielson, D. S. Smith, J. W. Kaminski, M. K. Kenney, and G. Peacock. "Health Care, Family, and Community Factors Associated with Mental, Behavioral, and Developmental Disorders and Poverty among Children Aged 2–8 Years—United States, 2016." *Morbidity and Mortality Weekly Report (MMWR)* 67, no. 5 (2018): 1377–83.

Danielson, M. L., R. H. Bitsko, R. M. Ghandour, J. R. Holbrook, and S. J. Blumberg. "Prevalence of Parent-Reported ADHD Diagnosis and Associated Treatment among U.S. Children and Adolescents, 2016." *Journal of Clinical Child and Adolescent Psychology* 47, no. 2 (March–April 2018): 199–212.

Data Resource Center for Child & Adolescent Health. "The National Survey of Children's Health." https://www.childhealthdata.org/learn-about-the-nsch/NSCH.

Davis-Laack, Paula. "Women & Happiness: Is It Still Declining?" *Psychology Today*, March 10, 2013, https://www.psychologytoday.com/us/blog/pressure-proof/201303/women-happiness-is-it-still-declining.

De Choudhury, Munmun, Michael Gamon, Scott Counts, and Eric Horvitz. "Predicting Depression via Social Media." Proceedings of the Seventh International AAAI Conference on Weblogs and Social Media, 2013, https://www.aaai.org/ocs/index.php/ICWSM/ICWSM13/paper/viewFile/6124/6351.

De Choudhury, Munmun, Scott Counts, and Michael Gamon. "Not All Moods Are Created Equal! Exploring Human Emotional States in Social Media." Proceedings of the Sixth International AAAI Conference on Weblogs and Social Media, 2012, https://www.aaai.org/ocs/index.php/ICWSM/ICWSM12/paper/download/4683/4968.

De Genna, Natacha M., Cynthia Larkby, and Marie D. Cornelius. "Pubertal Timing and Early Sexual Intercourse in the Offspring of Teenage Mothers." *Journal of Youth and Adolescence* 40, no. 10 (October 2011): 1315–28.

DeJean, Sarah L., Christi R. McGeorge, and Thomas Stone Carlson. "Attitudes Toward Never-Married Single Mothers and Fathers: Does Gender Matter?" *Journal of Feminist Family Therapy* 24, no. 2 (April 30, 2012): 121–38.

Diener, Ed. "Subjective Well-Being: The Science of Happiness and a Proposal for a National Index." *American Psychologist* 55, no. 1 (2000): 34–43.

———. "Subjective Well-Being." *Psychological Bulletin* 95, no. 3 (1984): 542–75.

Dishion, T. J., and L. D. Owen. "A Longitudinal Analysis of Friendships and Substance Use: Bidirectional Influence from Adolescence to Adulthood." *Developmental Psychology* 38, no. 4 (2002): 480–91.

Downing, J., and M. A. Bellis. "Early Pubertal Onset and Its Relationship with Sexual Risk Taking, Substance Use and Anti-Social Behavior: A Preliminary Cross-Sectional Study." *BMC Public Health* 9 (December 3, 2009): 446.

Downs, William R., and Brenda A. Miller. "Relationships between Experiences of Parental Violence during Childhood and Women's Psychiatric Symptomatology." *Journal of Interpersonal Violence* 13, no. 4 (August 1, 1998): 438–55.

Dryden-Edwards, Roxanne. "Teen Depression." *MedicineNet*, https://www.medicinenet.com/teen_depression/article.htm.

Dunn, A. L., M. H. Trivedi, and H. A. O'Neal. "Physical Activity Dose-Response Effects on Outcomes of Depression and Anxiety." *Medicine & Science in Sports & Exercise* 33, no. 6 (June 2001): S587–97, discussion 609-10.

East, L., D. Jackson, and L. O'Brien. "Disrupted Relationships: Adult Daughters and Father Absence." *Contemporary Nurse* 23, no. 2 (December 2006–January 2007): 252–61.

Ellis, Bruce J., and Judy Garber. "Psychosocial Antecedents of Variation in Girls' Pubertal Timing: Maternal Depression, Stepfather Presence, and Marital and Family Stress." *Child Development* 71, no. 2 (March–April 2000): 485–501.

Ellis, Bruce J., John E. Bates, Kenneth A. Dodge, David M. Fergusson, L. John Horwood, Gregory S. Pettit, and Lianne Woodward. "Does Father Absence Place Daughters at Special Risk for Early Sexual Activity and

Teenage Pregnancy?" *Child Development* 74, no. 3 (May–June 2003): 801–21.

Ellis, Sarah M., Yasmin S. Khan, Victor W. Harris, Ricki McWilliams, and Diana Converse. "The Impact of Fathers on Children's Well-Being." University of Florida IFAS Extension, September 2014, https://edis.ifas.ufl.edu/fy1451.

Elwood, David T., and Christopher Jencks. "The Spread of Single-Parent Families in the United States since 1960." John F. Kennedy School of Government Working Paper, Harvard University, February 2004, https://research.hks.harvard.edu/publications/getFile.aspx?Id=112.

Fabricius, William V. "Listening to Children of Divorce: New Findings That Diverge from Wallerstein, Lewis, and Blakeslee." *Family Relations: An Interdisciplinary Journal of Applied Family Studies* 52, no. 4 (2003): 385–96.

Faris, Stephanie. "Teenage Depression: Statistics, Symptoms, Diagnosis, and Treatments." Healthline newsletter, March 22, 2016, https://www.healthline.com/health/depression/teenage-depression.

Fetters, Ashley. "4 Big Problems with 'The Feminine Mystique.'" *The Atlantic*, Feb. 12, 2013, https://www.theatlantic.com/sexes/archive/2013/02/4-big-problems-with-the-feminine-mystique/273069/.

Fitzgerald, Joni F., and Robert C. "The Role of the Father in Anorexia. *Journal of Contemporary Psychotherapy* 30, no. 1 (March 2000): 71–84.

Flouri, Eirini. "Exploring the Relationships between Mothers' and Fathers' Parenting Practices and Children's Materialistic Values." *Journal of Economic Psychology* 25, no. 6 (February 2004): 743–52.

Frentz, C., F. M. Gresham, and S. N. Elliott. "Popular, Controversial, Neglected, and Rejected Adolescents: Contrasts of Social Competence and Achievement Differences." *Journal of School Psychology* 29, no. 2 (1991): 109–20.

Friedan, Betty. *The Second Stage*. Philippines: Summit Books, 1981.

Furman, W. F., and K. L. Bierman. "Children's Conceptions of Friendship: A Multi-Method Study of Developmental Changes." *Developmental Psychology* 20, no. 5 (1984): 925–31.

Gaunt, Ruth. "Biological Essentialism, Gender Ideologies, and Role Attitudes: What Determines Parents' Involvement in Child Care." *Sex Roles: A Journal of Research* 55, no. 7–8 (2006): 523–33.

General Social Survey. "Trends in Psychological Well-Being." NORC at the University of Chicago, April 2015, https://www.norc.org/PDFs/GSS%20Reports/GSS_PsyWellBeing15_final_formatted.pdf.

Ghandour, R. M., L. J. Sherman, C. J. Vladutiu, M. M. Ali, S. E. Lynch, R. H. Bitsko, and S. J. Blumberg. "Prevalence and Treatment of Depression, Anxiety, and Conduct Problems in U.S. Children." *Journal of Pediatrics* 206 (March 2019): 256–67.

Golden, Claudia, Lawrence F. Katz, and Ilyana Kuziemko. "The Homecoming of American College Women: The Reversal of the College Gender Gap." *Journal of Economic Perspectives* 20, no. 4 (2006): 133–56.

Grossmann, Karin, Klaus E. Grossmann, Elisabeth Fremmer-Bombik, Heinz Kindler, Hermann Scheuerer-Englisch, and Peter Zimmerman. "The Uniqueness of the Child-Father Attachment Relationship: Fathers' Sensitive and Challenging Play as a Pivotal Variable in a 16-Year Longitudinal Study." *Social Development* 11, no. 3 (July 11, 2002): 301–37.

Hauser, Stuart T. "Loevinger's Model and Measure of Ego Development: A Critical Review." *Psychological Bulletin* 83, no. 5 (1976): 928–55.

Hauser, Stuart T., E. B. Gerber, and J. P. Allen. "Ego Development and Attachment: Converging Platforms for Understanding Close Relationships." In *Personality Development: Theoretical, Empirical, and Clinical Implications of Loevinger's Conception of Ego Development*, edited by M. P. Westenberg and A. Blasi, 203–17. Mahwah, New Jersey: Lawrence Erlbaum Associates, 1998.

Hetherington, E. Mavis. "Effects of Father Absence on Personality Development in Adolescent Daughters." *Developmental Psychology* 7, no. 3 (1972): 313–26.

Hogan, Marjorie, and Victor Strasburg. "Body Image, Eating Disorders, and the Media." *Adolescent Medicine* 19 (2008): 1–27.

Hoier, Sabine. "Father Absence and Age at Menarche." *Human Nature* 14, no. 3 (September 2003): 209–33.

Huska, Liuan. "Has Attachment Parenting Theory Made Us Anxious Parents?" Christianity Today, July/August 2018, www.christianitytoday.com/women/2018/march/has-attachment-theory-made-us-anxious-parents.html.

Isen, Adam, and Betsey Stevenson. "Women's Education and Family Behavior: Trends in Marriage Divorce and Fertility." Working Paper, University of Pennsylvania, January 28, 2010.

Jeynes, William H. "The Effects of Recent Parental Divorce on Their Children's Consumption of Alcohol." *Journal of Youth and Adolescence* 30, no. 3 (June 2001): 305–19.

Jones, Kim A. "Assessing the Impact of Father-Absence from a Psychoanalytic Perspective." *Psychoanalytic Social Work* 14, no. 1 (2007): 43–58.

Kahneman, Daniel. "Objective Happiness." In *Well-Being: The Founda-tions of Hedonic Psychology*, by Daniel Kahneman, Ed Diener, and Norbert Schwarz, 3–25. New York: Russell Sage Foundation, 1999.

Khazan, Olga. "Fewer Sex Partners Means a Happier Marriage." *The Atlantic*, October 22, 2018, https://www.theatlantic.com/health/archive/2018/10/sexual-partners-and-marital-happiness/573493/.

Kilmann, Peter R., Laura V. Carranza, and Jennifer M. C. Vendemia. "Rec-ollections of Parent Characteristics and Attachment Patterns for College Women of Intact vs. Non-Intact Families." *Journal of Adolescence* 29, no. 1 (February 2006): 89–102.

Kimball, Miles, and Robert Willis. "Utility and Happiness." Mimeo, University of Michigan, October 30, 2006, http://www.econ.yale.edu/~shiller/behmacro/2006-11/kimball-willis.pdf.

Komisar, Erica. *Being There: Why Prioritizing Motherhood in the First Three Years Matters*. New York: TarcherPerigee, 2017.

Krohn, Franklin B., and Z. Bogan. "The Effects Absent Fathers Have on Female Development and College Attendance." *College Student Journal* 35 (2001): 598.

La Guardia, Amanda C., Judith A. Nelson, and Ian M. Lertora. "The Impact of Father Absence on Daughter Sexual Development and Behav-iors: Implications for Professional Counselors." *The Family Journal: Counseling and Therapy for Couples and Families* 22, no. 3 (2014): 339–46.

Lamb, Michael E., ed. *The Role of the Father in Child Development*. Hobo-ken, New Jersey: John Wiley, 2010.

Leavitt, Lewis. "Research to Practice: Emotional Development and Mater-nal/Infant Attachment." *Journal of Pediatric Health Care* 13, no. 3, Part 2 (May–June 1999): S4–S7.

Leckman J. F., and J. S. March. "Editorial: Developmental Neuroscience Comes of Age." *Journal of Child Psychology and Psychiatry* 52, no. 4 (April 2011): 333–8.

Leonard, Linda Schierse. *The Wounded Woman: Healing the Father-Daughter Relationship*. Boston: Shambhala, 1998.

Lewinsohn, P. M., P. Rohde, and J. R. Seeley. "Major Depressive Disorder in Older Adolescents: Prevalence, Risk Factors, and Clinical Implications." *Clinical Psychology Review* 18, no. 7 (November 1998): 765–94.

Lovell, Nancy. "God, Love, Sex, and the Meaning of Life: An Interview with Dr. Armand Nicholi." The High Calling,

February 14, 2006, https://www.theologyofwork.org/the-high-calling/blog/god-love-sex-and-meaning-life-interview-dr-armand-nicholi.

Marsh, Penny, Joseph P. Allen, Martin Ho, Maryfrances Porter, and F. Christy McFarland. "The Changing Nature of Adolescent Friendships Longitudinal Links with Early Adolescent Ego Development." *The Journal of Early Adolescence* 26, no. 4 (2006): 414–31.

McBride, Hillary L. *Mothers, Daughters and Body Image: Learning to Love Ourselves as We Are.* New York: Post Hill Press, 2017.

McIlhaney, Joe. *Hooked.* Chicago: Northfield Publishing, 2008.

Merck Newsroom Home. "FDA Approves Merck's HPV Vaccine, GARDASIL 9, to Prevent Cancers and Other Diseases Caused by Nine HPV Types- Including Types That Cause About 90% of Cervical Cancer Cases." December 11, 2014, https://www.mrknewsroom.com/news-release/prescription-medicine-news/fda-approves-mercks-hpv-vaccine-gardasil9-prevent-cancers-an.

Miller, Caroline. "Does Social Media Cause Depression: How Heavy Instagram and Facebook Use May Be Affecting Kids Negatively." Child Mind Institute, https://childmind.org/article/is-social-media-use-causing-depression/.

Minton, Carmelle, and Kay Pasley. "Fathers' Parenting Role Identity and Father Involvement: A Comparison of Nondivorced and Divorced, Nonresident Fathers." *Journal of Family Issues* 17, no. 1 (1996): 26–45.

Moffitt, T. E., A. Caspi, J. Belsky, and P. A. Silva. "Childhood Experience and the Onset of Menarche: A Test of a Sociobiological Model." *Child Development* 63, no. 1 (February 1992): 47–58.

Mojtabai, Ramin, Mark Olfson, and Beth Han. "National Trends in the Prevalence and Treatment of Depression in Adolescents and Young Adults." *Pediatrics* 138, no. 6 (December 2016), https://pediatrics.aappublications.org/content/138/6/e20161878.

Moreno, Megan A., Lauren A. Jelenchick, Katie G. Egan, Elizabeth Cox, Henry Young, Kerry E. Gannon, and Tara Becker. "Feeling Bad on Facebook: Depression Disclosures by College Students on a Social Networking Site." *Depression and Anxiety* 28, no. 6 (June 2011): 447–55.

Munsey, Christopher. "Does Marriage Make Us Happy?" *American Psychological Association* 41, no. 9 (October 2010): https://www.apa.org/monitor/2010/10/marriage.

National Institute of Mental Health. "Major Depression." https://www.nimh.nih.gov/health/statistics/major-depression.shtml.

National Survey on Drug Use and Health (NSDUH), https://nsduhweb.rti. org/respweb/homepage.cfm.

Newland, Lisa A., and Diana D. Coyl-Shepherd. "Fathers' Role as Attachment Figure: An Interview with Sir Richard Bowlby." *Early Child Development and Care* 180, no. 1–2 (January 2010): 25–32.

Nicholi, Armand M. *The Harvard Guide to Modern Psychiatry.* Cambridge, Massachusetts: Belknap Press of Harvard University Press, 1978.

_____. *The Question of God: C.S. Lewis and Sigmund Freud Debate God, Love, Sex, and the Meaning of Life.* New York: Free Press, 2002.

Nielsen, Linda. "Divorced Fathers and Their Daughters: A Review of Recent Research." *Journal of Divorce & Remarriage* 52, no. 2 (February 10, 2011): 77–93.

O'Donnell, Jayne, and Anne Saker. "Teen Suicide Is Soaring. Do Spotty Mental Health and Addiction Treatment Share Blame?" *USA Today*, March 19, 2018, https://www.usatoday.com/story/news/politics/2018/03/19/ teen-suicide-soaring-do-spotty-mental-health-and-addiction-treatment-share-blame/428148002/.

O'Keeffe, Gwenn Schurgin, and Kathleen Clarke-Pearson. "The Impact of Social Media on Children, Adolescents, and Families." *American Academy of Pediatrics* 127, no. 4 (April 2011): 800–4, https://pediat-rics.aappublications.org/content/127/4/800.

Oates, R. Kim, Douglas Forrest, and Anthony Peacock. "Self-Esteem of Abused Children." *Child Abuse & Neglect* 9, no. 2 (1985): 159–63.

Olson, K. R., L. Durwood, M. DeMeules, and K. A. McLaughlin. "Mental Health of Transgender Children Who Are Supported in Their Identities." *Pediatrics* 137, no. 3 (March 2016): http://pediatrics.aappublications.org/content/137/3/e20153223 pmid:26921285.

Parents Television Council. "The New Media: The Wild Wild West." Facts and TV Statistics, https://w2.parentstv.org/main/Research/Facts.aspx.

Perkins, Rose Merlino. "The Father-Daughter Relationship: Familial Interactions That Impact a Daughter's Style of Life." *College Student Journal* 35, no. 4 (2001): 616–26.

Perou, R., R. H. Bitsko, S. J. Blumberg, P. Pastor, R. M. Ghandour, J. C. Gfroerer, S. L. Hedden, A. E. Crosby, S. N. Visser, L. A. Schieve, S. E. Parks, J. E. Hall, D. Brody, C. M. Simile, W. W. Thompson, J. Baio, S. Avenevoli, M. D. Kogan, and L. N. Huang. "Mental Health Surveillance among Children—United States, 2005–2011." *Morbidity and Mortality Weekly Report (MMWR)* 62, no. 2 (May 17, 2013): 1–35.

Petherick, Anna. "Gains in Women's Rights Haven't Made Women Happier. Why Is That?" *The Guardian*, May 18, 2016, https://www.theguardian.com/lifeandstyle/2016/may/18/womens-rights-happiness-wellbeing-gender-gap.

Pew Research Center. "The Decline of Marriage and Rise of New Families." November 18, 2010, https://www.pewsocialtrends.org/wp-content/uploads/sites/3/2010/11/pew-social-trends-2010-families.pdf.

Pezzini, Silvia. "The Effect of Women's Rights on Women's Welfare: Evidence from a Natural Experiment." *The Economic Journal* 115, no. 502 (March 2, 2005): C208–27.

Pfefferle S. G., and E. L. Spitznagel. "Children's Mental Health Service Use and Maternal Mental Health: A Path Analytic Model." *Children and Youth Services Review* 31, no. 3 (March 2009): 378–82.

Pleck, Joseph H. "Paternal Involvement: Revised Conceptualization and Theoretical Linkages with Child Outcomes." In *The Role of the Father in Child Development*, edited by M. E. Lamb, 66–104. New York: John Wiley, 2010.

Posner, Rachel Blumstein. "Early Menarche: A Review of Research on Trends in Timing, Racial Differences, Etiology, and Psychosocial Consequences." *Sex Roles: A Journal of Research* 54, no. 5–6 (2006): 315–22.

Pullmann, Joy. "The Feminist Life Script Has Made Many Women Miserable. Don't Let It Sucker You." The Federalist, December 11, 2018, https://thefederalist.com/2018/12/11/the-feminist-life-script-has-made-many-women-miserable-dont-let-it-sucker-you/.

Raeburn, Paul. "How Dads Influence Teens' Happiness." Scientific American Mind Behavior & Society, May 1, 2014, https://www.scientificamerican.com/article/how-dads-influence-teens-happiness/.

Roberts, Daniel F., Ulla G. Foehr, and Victoria Rideout. "Generation M2: Media in the Lives of 8–18-Year-Olds." Kaiser Family Foundation, 2010, https://www.kff.org/wp-content/uploads/2013/04/8010.pdf.

____. "Generation M: Media in the Lives of 8–18-Year-Olds." Kaiser Family Foundation, March 2005, https://www.kff.org/wp-content/uploads/2013/01/generation-m-media-in-the-lives-of-8-18-year-olds-report.pdf.

Robertson, Matra. *Starving in the Silences: An Exploration of Anorexia Nervosa*. Washington Square: New York University Press, 1992.

Robinson, Matthew S., and Lauren B. Alloy. "Negative Cognitive Styles and Stress-Reactive Rumination Interact to Predict Depression: A Prospective Study." *Cognitive Therapy and Research* 27, no. 3 (June 2003): 275–91.

Sax, Leonard. *Boys Adrift: The Five Factors Driving the Growing Epidemic of Unmotivated Boys and Underachieving Young Men.* New York: Basic Books, 2016.

____. *Girls on the Edge.* New York: Basic Books, 2010.

____. *The Collapse of Parenting: How We Hurt Our Kids When We Treat Them Like Grown-Ups.* New York: Basic Books, 2016.

____. *Why Gender Matters, Second Edition: What Parents and Teachers Need to Know about the Emerging Science of Sex and Differences.* New York: Harmony Books, 2017.

Secunda, Victoria. *Women and Their Fathers.* New York: Bantam Double-day Dell, 1992.

Soltanian, Ali Reza, Amiri Mohammad, Soudabeh Namazi, Hossein Qaedi, and Gholam Reza Kohan. "Mental Health Changes and Its Predictors in Adolescents Using the Path Analytic Model: A 7-Year Observational Study." *Iranian Journal of Psychiatry* 9, no. 1 (March 2014): 1–7.

Stanford Children's Health. "Teen Suicide." https://www.stanfordchildrens. org/en/topic/default?id=teen-suicide-90-P02584.

Steinem, Gloria. *Revolution from Within: A Book of Self-Esteem.* New York: Little, Brown and Company, 1993.

Steingard, Ron J. "Mood Disorders and Teenage Girls: Why They Are More Vulnerable Than Boys, and What Signs and Symptoms You Should Look For." Child Mind Institute, https://childmind.org/article/ mood-disorders-and-teenage-girls/.

Stevenson, Betsey, and Justin Wolfers. "Happiness Inequality in the United States." *Journal of Legal Studies* 37, no. S2 (2008): 33–79.

____. "Marriage and Divorce: Changes and Their Driving Forces." *Journal of Economic Perspectives* 21, no. 2 (2007): 27–52.

____. "The Paradox of Declining Female Happiness." NBER (National Bureau of Economic Research) Working Paper No. 14969, May 2009, https://www.nber.org/papers/w14969.pdf.

Sugarman, Joe. "The Rise of Teen Depression." *Johns Hopkins Health Review* 4, no. 2 (Fall/Winter 2017), https://www.johnshopkinshealthre-view.com/issues/fall-winter-2017/articles/the-rise-of-teen-depression.

Tither, J. M., and B. J. Ellis. "Impact of Fathers on Daughters' Age at Men-arche: A Genetically and Environmentally Controlled Sibling Study." *Developmental Psychology* 44, no. 5 (2008): 1409–20.

Twenge, Jean M. "The Age of Anxiety? Birth Cohort Change in Anxiety and Neuroticism, 1952-1993." *Journal of Personality and Social Psychology* 79, no. 6 (2000): 1007–21.

Visser, Susanna N., Melissa L. Danielson, Rebecca H. Bitsko, Ruth Perou, and Stephen J. Blumberg. "Convergent Validity of Parent-reported ADHD Diagnosis: A Cross-study Comparison." *JAMA Pediatrics* 167, no. 7 (July 2013): 674–5.

Wedge, Marilyn. "Why French Kids Don't Have ADHD." *Psychology Today*, March 8, 2012, https://www.psychologytoday.com/us/blog/suffer-the-children/201203/why-french-kids-dont-have-adhd.

Wilcox, Bradford. "The Distinct, Positive Impact of a Good Dad: How Fathers Contribute to Their Kids' Lives." *The Atlantic*, June 14, 2013, theatlantic.com/sexes/archive/2013/06/the-distinct-positive-impact-of-a-good-dad/276874.

Zacharias, Ravi. "'Who Are You, Really?' – A Dr. Ravi Zacharias Presentation." YouTube, March 23, 2013, https://www.youtube.com/watch?v=er0vbK2xKN0.

____. "RZIM: Life's Four Big Questions, Q and A – by Ravi Zacharias @ University of Kentucky." YouTube, June 2, 2016, https://www.youtube.com/watch?v=DseIM5MlpS0.

Zagorski, Nick. "Using Many Social Media Platforms Linked with Depression, Anxiety Risk." Psychiatric News, January 17, 2017, https://psychnews.psychiatryonline.org/doi/10.1176/appi.pn.2017.1b16.

Notes

Chapter One: Know Her Heart

1. Courtney Ackerman, "What is Attachment Theory? Bowlby's 4 Stages Explained," PositivePsychology.com, April 27, 2018, https://positive psychology.com/attachment-theory/#definition.
2. Ibid.
3. Leonard Sax, *Why Gender Matters, Second Edition: What Parents and Teachers Need to Know about the Emerging Science of Sex Differences* (New York: Doubleday, 2017).
4. Harold G. Koenig, "Religion, Spirituality, and Health: The Research and Clinical Implications," *ISRN Psychiatry*, December 16, 2012, https://www.ncbi.nlm.nih.gov/pmc/articles/PMC3671693/.
5. Rachel K. Narr et al., "Close Friendship Strength and Broader Peer Group Desirability as Differential Predictors of Adult Mental Health," *Child Development*, August 21, 2017, https://onlinelibrary.wiley.com/doi/full/10.1111/cdev.12905.
6. Aristotle, *Nichomachean Ethics*, trans. Robert C. Bartlett and Susan D. Collins (Chicago: University of Chicago Press, 2012).
7. Shelley E. Taylor et al., "Biobehavioral Responses to Stress in Females: Tend-and-Befriend, Not Fight-or-Flight," *Psychological Review* 107, no. 3 (2000): 411–29, https://taylorlab.psych.ucla.edu/wp-content/uploads/sites/5/2014/10/2000_Biobehavioral-responses-to-stress-in-females_tend-and-befriend.pdf.

Chapter Two: Answer Her Four Biggest Questions

1. Ravi Zacharias, "Four Questions to Answer in Life–Dr. Ravi Zacharias," YouTube, December 10, 2014, https://www.youtube.com/watch?v=Hfb5-7mtC-8.
2. C. S. Lewis, *God in the Dock* (Grand Rapids, Michigan: Eerdmans, 2001), 211.
3. Henry Cloud and John Townsend, *Boundaries: When To Say Yes, How To Say No To Take Control of Your Life* (Grand Rapids, Michigan: Zondervan, 2017).

Chapter Three: Mom: Mentor, Ally, Glue

1. Erica Komisar, *Being There: Why Prioritizing Motherhood in the First Three Years Matters* (New York: TarcherPerigee, 2017).

2. For an example of a book that applies lessons from novels to real life, see Elizabeth Kantor, *The Jane Austen Guide to Happily Ever After* (Washington, D.C.: Regnery, 2012). There are many others.
3. Komisar, *Being There*, 146–47.

Chapter Four: Dads: Be Her First Love, Protector, amd Leader

1. I summarize these findings in my book *Strong Fathers, Strong Daughters: 10 Secrets Every Father Should Know* (Washington, D.C.: Regnery, 2015).
2. Binta Alleyne-Green et al., "Father Involvement, Dating Violence, and Sexual Risk Behaviors Among a National Sample of Adolescent Females," *Journal of Interpersonal Violence*, December 3, 2014, https://www.ncbi.nlm.nih.gov/pmc/articles/PMC5007216/.

Chapter Five: Help Her Take Control of Screens

1. Yvonne Kelly et al., "Social Media Use and Adolescent Mental Health: Findings From the UK Millennium Cohort Study," *EClinicalMedicine*, January 4, 2019, https://www.thelancet.com/journals/eclinm/article/PIIS2589-5370(18)30060-9/fulltext.
2. Melissa G. Hunt et al., "No More FOMO: Limiting Social Media Decreases Loneliness and Depression," *Journal of Social and Clinical Psychology* 37, no. 10 (November 2018): 751–68.
3. Nancy Jo Sales, *American Girls: Social Media and the Secret Lives of Teenagers* (New York: Alfred A. Knopf, 2016).
4. Sherry Turkle, *Alone Together: Why We Expect More from Technology and Less from Each Other* (New York: Basic Books, 2011).

Chapter Six: Teach Her Healthy versus Toxic Feminism

1. Betty Friedan, *The Second Stage* (Cambridge, Massachusetts: Harvard University Press, 1998), 84.
2. Betsey Stevenson and Justin Wolfers, "The Paradox of Declining Female Happiness," National Bureau of Economic Research, Working Paper 14969, May 2009, https://www.nber.org/papers/w14969.

Chapter Seven: Eating, Body Image, and Helping Our Daughters Strike the Right Balance

1. Seeta Pai and Kelly Schryver, "Children, Teens, Media, and Body Image: A Common Sense Media Research Brief," Common Sense Media, January 21, 2015, https://www.commonsensemedia.org/research/children-teens-media-and-body-image.

2. Seeta Pai and Kelly Schryver, "Children, Teens, Media, and Body Image Infographic," Common Sense Media, January 20, 2015, https://www.commonsensemedia.org/children-teens-body-image-media-infographic.
3. Eating Disorder Foundation, https://www.eatingdisorderfoundation.org/.
4. "Eating Disorder Statistics," National Association of Anorexia Nervosa and Associated Disorders, https://anad.org/education-and-awareness/about-eating-disorders/eating-disorders-statistics/.
5. Eating Disorder Foundation, "Statistics: Eating Disorders and Their Precursors," Creighton University, https://www.creighton.edu/fileadmin/user/StudentServices/StudentSuccess/EatingDisorderStatistics.pdf.
6. Beth A. Abramovitz and Leann L. Birch, "Five-Year-Old Girls' Ideas about Dieting Are Predicted by Their Mothers' Dieting," *Journal of the American Dietetic Association* 100, no. 10 (2000): 1157–63, https://www.ncbi.nlm.nih.gov/pmc/articles/PMC2530935/.
7. Craig M. Hales et al., "Prevalence of Obesity among Adults and Youth: United States, 2015–2016," Data Brief No. 288, National Center for Health Statistics, October 2017, https://www.cdc.gov/nchs/products/databriefs/db288.htm.
8. For instance, see: Caroline Miller, "Does Social Media Cause Depression?" Child Mind Institute, https://childmind.org/article/is-social-media-use-causing-depression/.

Chapter Eight: Root Her Faith in God

1. Harold G. Koenig, "Religion, Spirituality, and Health: The Research and Clinical Implications," *ISRN Psychiatry*, December 16, 2012, https://www.ncbi.nlm.nih.gov/pmc/articles/PMC3671693/.
2. For more on this, see Rick Warren's groundbreaking book *The Purpose Driven Life: What on Earth Am I Here For?* (Grand Rapids, Michigan: Zondervan, 2012).
3. Saint Augustine, *The Confessions of Saint Augustine*, trans. John K. Ryan, (New York: Doubleday, 1988), 1.
4. Peter Kreeft and Ronald K. Tacelli, *Handbook of Christian Apologetics* (Westmont, Illinois: InterVarsity Press, 1994), 22.

Chapter Nine: Help Her Develop a Healthy Sexuality

1. Centers for Disease Control and Prevention, "Sexual Risk Behaviors Can Lead to HIV, STDs, & Teen Pregnancy," https://www.cdc.gov/healthyyouth/sexualbehaviors/index.htm.
2. HealthyPeople.gov, "Sexually Transmitted Diseases," https://www.healthypeople.gov/2020/topics-objectives/topic/sexually-transmitted-diseases.

3. Centers for Disease Control and Prevention, "Adolescents and Young Adults," https://www.cdc.gov/std/life-stages-populations/adolescents-youngadults.htm.
4. Centers for Disease Control and Prevention, "One in Four Teenage Girls in U.S. Has Sexually Transmitted Disease, CDC Study Shows," ScienceDaily, March 12, 2008, https://www.sciencedaily.com/releases/2008/03/080312084645.htm.
5. Kari P. Braaten and Marc R. Laufer, "Human Papillomavirus (HPV), HPV-Related Disease, and the HPV Vaccine," *Reviews in Obstetrics & Gynecology* 1, no. (Winter 2008), https://www.ncbi.nlm.nih.gov/pmc/articles/PMC2492590/.
6. World Health Organization, "Human Papillomavirus (HPV) and Cervical Cancer," January 24, 2019, https://www.who.int/news-room/fact-sheets/detail/human-papillomavirus-(hpv)-and-cervical-cancer.
7. Centers for Disease Control and Prevention, "Chlamydia – CDC Fact Sheet (Detailed)," https://www.cdc.gov/std/chlamydia/stdfact-chlamydia-detailed.htm.
8. Centers for Disease Control and Prevention, "Gonorrhea," https://www.cdc.gov/std/stats17/gonorrhea.htm.
9. Danielle G. Tsevat et al., "Sexually Transmitted Diseases and Infertility," *American Journal of Obstetrics and Gynecology* 216, no. 1 (January 2017): 1–9, https://www.ncbi.nlm.nih.gov/pmc/articles/PMC5193130/.
10. HealthyPeople.gov, "Sexually Transmitted Diseases."
11. Avert, "Women and Girls, HIV and AIDS," https://www.avert.org/professionals/hiv-social-issues/key-affected-populations/women.
12. Sally Law, "Survey Finds 'Friends with Benefits' Common," Live Science, April 2, 2009, https://www.livescience.com/5391-survey-finds-friends-benefits-common.html.
13. Joe S. McIlhaney Jr. and Freda McKissic Bush, *Hooked: New Science on How Casual Sex Is Affecting Our Children* (Chicago: Northfield Publishing, 2008).
14. Joe Sugarman, "The Rise of Teen Depression," *Johns Hopkins Health Review* 4, no. 2 (Fall/Winter 2017), https://www.johnshopkinshealthreview.com/issues/fall-winter-2017/articles/the-rise-of-teen-depression.

Chapter Ten: Help Her Find Good Friends (and Deal with the Bad Ones)

1. National Institute of Mental Health, "Any Anxiety Disorder," https://www.nimh.nih.gov/health/statistics/any-anxiety-disorder.shtml.

2.   Rachel K. Narr et al., "Close Friendship Strength and Broader Peer Group
      Desirability as Differential Predictors of Adult Mental Health," *Child
      Development* 90, no. 1 (August 21, 2017), https://onlinelibrary.wiley.com/
      doi/full/10.1111/cdev.12905.
3.   Society for Research in Child Development, "Close Friendships in High
      School Predict Improvements in Mental Health in Young Adulthood,"
      Science Daily, August 22, 2017, https://www.sciencedaily.com/
      releases/2017/08/170822092221.htm.
4.   Tom Rath, *Vital Friends: The People You Can't Afford to Live Without*
      (Washington, D.C.: Gallup Press, 2006), 24; Jane Collingwood, "The
      Importance of Friendship," Psych Central, March 18, 2019, https://
      psychcentral.com/lib/the-importance-of-friendship/.
5.   Gale Berkowitz, "UCLA Study on Friendship Among Women," Anapsid.
      org, 2002, http://www.anapsid.org/cnd/gender/tendfend.html.

Chapter Eleven: Help Her Be a Strong Woman, Not a Victim

1.   Charles J. Sykes, *A Nation of Victims: The Decay of the American
      Character* (New York: St. Martin's Press, 1992).
2.   C. S. Lewis, *The Chronicles of Narnia* (New York: HarperCollins, 1956),
      511.

Index